H A R P S
in the
WILLOWS

HARPS
in the
WILLOWS

Strengths for
Reinventing Life

NAOMI MITCHUM

Chalice Press®
St. Louis, Missouri

All scripture quotations, unless otherwise indicated, are from the *New Revised Standard Version Bible*, copyright 1989, Division of Christian Education of the National Council of the Churches of Christ in the USA. Used by permission.

Scriptures marked (Phillips) are reprinted by permission of Simon & Schuster, from the *New Testament in Modern English*, revised edition, translated by J. B. Phillips. © 1958, 1960, 1972 by J. B. Phillips.

Scripture quotations marked (NIV) are taken from the HOLY BIBLE, NEW INTERNATIONAL VERSION®. NIV®. Copyright © 1973, 1978, 1984 by International Bible Society. Used by permission of Zondervan Publishing House. All rights reserved.

Words to "God Is Here" by Fred Pratt Green.Words © 1979 Hope Publishing Company, Carol Stream, IL 60188. All rights reserved. Used by permission.

Cover art: PhotoDisc image, computer enhanced by Lynne Condellone
Cover design: Lynne Condellone
Interior design: Elizabeth Wright
Art direction: Elizabeth Wright

This book is printed on acid-free, recycled paper.

Visit Chalice Press on the World Wide Web at
www.chalicepress.com

10 9 8 7 6 5 4 3 2 1   01 02 03 04 05 06

Library of Congress Cataloging–in–Publication Data

Mitchum, Naomi.
   Harps in the willows : strengths for reinventing life / Naomi Mitchum.
    p.   cm.
   Includes bibliographical references and index.
   ISBN 0-8272-1440-5
   1. Christian life.   2. Life change events—Religious aspects—Christianity.
I. Title.
BV4501.2 .M542 2001
248.4— dc21   2001000778

TABLE OF CONTENTS

Introduction to
REINVENTION

This book is about building strength and hope in the midst of fast-moving, gut-wrenching life experiences that bring us up short and leave us gasping. It's about making decisions for Change with a capital C, the Change for which we're not quite prepared.

Change is desirable and inevitable, happening in a steady flow and requiring so little effort that we observe it, at the time, simply as solving a small problem or taking advantage of an opportunity. With only minor glitches, each of us develops coping skills that allow us to learn to adapt to natural changes.

Then suddenly a life-altering event grabs us by the scruff of the neck and shakes us until we feel like a tired puppy. The event eats up energy and saps our time and money as we scramble to understand what's happening. Confused and feeling inadequate, we find ourselves in grief for what we have lost and in fear of what is ahead. Old coping patterns simply aren't working, and we feel the pain of realization that we must make accommodations and invent a new lifestyle that matches what is happening to us.

A calamitous, life-altering event may be as simple as a sudden move to another city, or it may be of catastrophic proportions, such as:

- Imminent death
- The death of a family member or close friend
- The birth of a physically or mentally impaired child
- Becoming a long-term caregiver
- The diagnosis of a chronic illness
- Mental illness in the family
- The diagnosis of a catastrophic illness
- Discrimination

- Violence
- The shell of your burned home
- Discovering that a child has leukemia or AIDS
- A sudden, jolting discovery that your life has been misspent
- Divorce and/or losing a custody battle

If you have experienced these or similar events, rest assured that life can once again have balance and peace. You can learn to adapt to change as you reinvent your way of life from day to day, week to week, and year to year. You may long for, pray for, even wait for a "quick-fix" healing of wounds caused by life-altering events, but if the fix doesn't seem to appear, you can roll up your sleeves and take on the role of *reinventor* for your own life.

Becoming the Reinventor

As an inventor, and by necessity a reinventor, you are in good company. Many real-life inventions were spawned by necessity. For example, Louis Braille, blinded at an early age, was sent to the French Institute for the Blind. As a young student he played with a series of raised dots the army used for night code, using it to send notes to his dormitory friends at night. Although it took him years to perfect the new system, he later published a sophisticated writing system of six raised dots. Louis Braille also had the benefit of a system proposed by Valentin Hany some years earlier, so in some ways Louis Braille *re*-invented an easier way to read with the fingertips.[1]

Most people knew him as a statesman and writer, but farmers knew Thomas Jefferson as the person who reinvented a plow board that cut a deeper furrow with much less effort. His plow, however, was soon replaced by an all-iron plow that was even more efficient.[2]

J. S. Bach reinvented musically! From his heart and mind he created a melody of touching beauty that he then changed with frills and variations, making it over, twisting and changing his original musical line into ever-new-sounding combinations. When you go to an organ concert and hear a Bach fugue, you will hear his reinvention of a melody line.

Necessity

In many ways inventing and reinventing *things* such as raised dots, plows, and music is different from reinventing a life, but there are great similarities. First, although we all have our comfort zones in the ways we operate our lives, often there is a built-in quest for doing things better or differently, a way to keep life creative and interesting. Second, when old ways are inadequate, sudden necessity forces us to find a fresh approach, and new coping skills are born. Third, whether it's Braille, plows, music, or a life, nothing is permanent; everything is always under reconstruction. The challenge of change gives us second, third, even unlimited chances for reinvention—and, as in Braille's case, the reinvention may go on for years.

Fourth, it is not enough just to survive. Most people want to wring "real life" out of living, even if it must be done in a new way. Because there are no road maps with arrows pointing to "real life—this way" or "get your balance—this way" we have the opportunity to accommodate and reinvent as Louis Braille did. Reinvention is a "must," but it is also an opportunity and an adventure.

Deep Strength

Being propelled into making sudden life decisions involves unfamiliar issues with family, friends, and coworkers. As we search for the next sure footing in our lives, it is hard for us to tell fellow travelers our innermost thoughts, and we cry out for someone to walk the new road with us. If we are fortunate, an understanding friend or relative will put an arm around our shoulder and listen. However, the most important strength for reinventing life during Change comes from a loving God who always aids, sustains, inspires, and heals.

The essays in this book are stories of personal journeys with this steadfast, loving God. The essays are all mine, with illustrations used by permission. They record peaks and valleys in my own experiences as a caregiver and care receiver. They also reflect, by necessity, my thoughts as a person called on to make fast changes in life's direction because of unusual events. Although mine is a Christian perspective, the reinvention journey is open to many other forms of spiritual help and various other belief systems.

The writings are not meant to be do-it-yourself formulas. They are a simple sharing of how positive lifestyle and spiritual growth can help a person accommodate to allow for Change— an attitude of "Come here, let me tell you how this works for me." Many of the essays were written for the chronic illness support groups at Chapelwood United Methodist Church in Houston, Texas. Others were given as devotionals for church and community groups. Everywhere I spoke, there was a gift exchange as persons shared their stories, spiritual insights, and coping skills, so, in a sense, persons from these groups have contributed ideas and helped refine the reflections, and they have encouraged me to put them into print.

I

Reinventing
LIFESTYLE

In the face of great Change, the questions we ask and the answers we seek may cause us to change our lifestyle. In fact, the event itself may have already caused radical changes in the way we spend our time, money, and energy. This section offers ideas for developing new attitudes and coping skills that will help us take charge of what is happening to us.

Lifestyle may be defined as the reflection of our beliefs about ourselves, our universe, our God, and those around us into the daily focus of life. From this reflection our actual style for living is born. Our attitudes toward life are mirrored in this comfort zone or style of life. In many ways we may be called to look at life differently and make a major attitude adjustment that will help us reinvent an appropriate lifestyle.

Harps in the Willows

There We Sat Down

There are times in our lives when we want to sit down and cry. Tears, often a plea for help, wash down some frustrations and disappointments. Other frustrations just sit there beside us, refusing to budge. After a while, we don't have time to sit. We have to strike out and do something, right or wrong. It has happened to me and to others you will read about in this book.

Discovery

It's official. After a second and even a third opinion, you really do have a serious disease. A paralysis of fear climbs through your nervous system. Before driving home from the doctor's office, you go to the building's coffee shop to sit for a while as you try to absorb what is happening. You're numb, and everything around you begins to look blurred. You may never be well again. Jumping to both true and imagined conclusions makes outlandish ideas and contradictions whirl inside your brain. You start naming your imagined losses, and the whirl goes so deep you force your attention to something else. It's grief and anger wrapped in numbing denial. Three cups of coffee later, the numbness persists, but somehow you drive home.

A few miles away your friend has just received a paralyzing phone call telling him that his intoxicated seventeen-year-old son ran his car into a van. Three persons in the van were killed. Numb with shock, your friend hurries to the hospital to check on his son, only to find a policeman guarding the door. The son, now in need of permanent medical care, will also require money for lawyers and may spend his life in prison.

Days and weeks of time grind by. Bad news is always just behind the eyes. If a friend asks how you are feeling, tears well up and spill down your cheeks. At church when you try to sing, the sound gets stuck in your throat. You may never sing again. When you talk to God for comfort, there seems to be only strange silence. Now begin the fervent questions: Where is God? How could God let this occur? Why am I so upset? With God's help I should be strong enough to handle this, so why am I confused and afraid?

Then the guilt questions come: "Did I cause this illness by being spiritually weak? Am I being punished for. . . ?" You may sink lower in an ocean of questions. Or perhaps you think you have a handle on your emotions until new questions come. Beliefs and disbelief swirl in your head, and even deeper fears set in. Medical terms and new limitations challenge your thinking and lifestyle. Inside, a voice says, "I don't know what's happening to me. I feel like I'm an exile in a new land where I don't speak the language."

Your friend is asking the same kinds of questions with slight variations. "Should I have been more strict with my son?" Or he might be asking questions about his own drinking. The foremost question is, "Who will take care of this impaired child? I must work." Then comes the legal morass, a new set of rules, a new language with double-speak. Inside, a voice says, "I feel like an exile in a new land where I don't speak the language."

In the land of exile there are concerns for other losses, such as your family, livelihood, way of life, or self-esteem. Losses are all different, and at first they may not be rational, but they are still to be suffered until they are sorted. Sorting is part of the grief process, and grief is necessary and inevitable if you want to move on with your life.

Permission to Grieve

An Old Testament Bible story may give you a permission slip for a time of grief, and it may guide you to make accommodations in your way of life. Here is a sketch of the Bible story.:

It's 586 B.C.E., and the Judeans are in shock. The majestic temple in Jerusalem has been burned down by a foreign army that also sacked their homes. The temple has been the holy place of worship and sacrifice, which defined their community and personal lives, and it is the place where they believe God exists. Even the sight of the burned-out rubble is incomprehensible. How could God let this happen?

Feeling abandoned by God, many Judeans are herded like cattle to the country of Babylonia. Separated from their families and the comfort zones of their lives, they are forced into an unfamiliar culture with a strange language and even stranger laws. While mourning, they must make accommodations and impossible adaptations. Reaction to life in the city of Babylon is mixed, but the Judeans are in grief. A psalmist later tells of their reaction as their captors taunt them:

> By the rivers of Babylon—
>> there we sat down and there we wept
>> when we remembered Zion.
> On the willows there
>> we hung up our harps.
> For there our captors
>> asked us for songs,
> and our tormentors asked for mirth, saying,
>> "Sing us one of the songs of Zion!"
> How could we sing the LORD's song
>> in a foreign land? (Ps. 137:1–4)

The Judeans grieved! They would never again play their harps and sing. Hanging their harps in the willow trees became an act of final desolation. Their God seemed silent. They were silent. Joy was gone.

Inclination to Reinvent

But as time passed, they made new lives for themselves, and they made the astounding discovery that God was not dead in the ashes they had left in Jerusalem. Tentatively, they stepped into a way of thinking that would revolutionize their lives: *God had run in their past, they reasoned. Why would God not walk with them in the future?*

A group began to gather to hear the elders recite from memory portions of God's word that had been written on scrolls destroyed in the temple. Out of their gathering, the synagogue was born. It became a center for worship, instruction, and prayer. Jewish scribes began to write out what they could remember of God's word, giving the synagogues and people sacred scrolls once again.

Grief had become their teacher. And the power of grief and eternal seeking after God had become inventive. Many of the Judeans rediscovered God and once again looked to a full life ahead of them. They found a future, and they did learn to sing again. Figuratively, they even picked up their discarded harps from the willows.

The Move to Reinvent

When God seems silent and joy seems gone, when your soul feels parched, when you feel like hanging your singing harp in the willows, grief can become a teacher, and the shock of change can move you to reinvent.

Grief is inevitable, a part of the normal process of life and not reserved only for the death of a loved one. Other griefs beset us at many turns, from diagnosis of an illness or becoming entangled in an automobile accident to divorce, loss of custody, becoming a permanent caregiver, or losing our possessions. The mourning for losses in these and other events occurs in patterns. Although the patterns vary with individuals, most grief begins with a state of shock, perhaps God's way of making the initial event bearable for a while. Then, following varying routes, a person's emotions seek expression through loneliness, sadness, anxiety, panic, anger, guilt, resentment, or hope. During these times, life may seem out of balance; the comfort zone for daily life stays elusive. After a while comforting balance comes, and then the inclination to continue, to just have a life. And, appearing sporadically but finally winning out, comes the inclination to reinvent a satisfying style of life, one that can be lived with zest.

Working through grief isn't easy, but it can lead you to discovery and growth. Coping styles vary with individuals, so the speed at which persons grow into different stages of grief will vary. A comforting God never abandons at any stage of the grief process but can put in your heart the inclination to reinvent a life accommodated to any event requiring change. Only you can choose the right time to recognize and act on this inclination. Only you can become an inventor of your own new and adventuresome lifestyle.

Just as God walked with the Hebrews into the future, God will walk, even run, with you in the future.

The psalmists who spoke so eloquently of their inner longings and feelings looked to the future and requested, in the form of a prayer, that light and truth would lead them. Psalm 43 begins with a prayer for deliverance and moves into promises of praise:

> O send out your light and your truth;
>   let them lead me;
> let them bring me to your holy hill
>   and to your dwelling.
> Then I will go to the altar of God,
>   to God my exceeding joy;
> and I will praise you with the harp,
>   O God, my God. (Ps. 43:3–4)

More reading on this subject is available.

If you think you are the only one who sinks into the mire of grief, self-pity, ambivalence, and doubt, think again. It has been done by experts. The Old Testament is filled with stories of persons who picked up their harps and sang again when they reinvented their lives. Read some of the following Psalms: 13, 42, 57, 61, 70, 73, 86, 143.

Read about the emptiness of life for Naomi when her husband and sons died. The story of how she reinvented a life is found in the book of Ruth. Or read the gospels, especially Luke and John, or the book of Acts to discover how grief-stricken disciples followed their inclinations after Jesus' death to reinvest themselves in what he had taught.

Down to the Scrap Pile

One of the highlights of taking my family to visit my parents in a small Kansas town was going to the wonderful, odorous municipal dump. Smoke wafted from the center of the trash and garbage, and at the periphery were assorted furniture, car parts, window frames, fans, and other discards. A glorious place for scavengers! My father, a municipal dump scavenger himself, passed this recreational activity to me. I have always had a nose for redeeming junk, so I enjoyed going with Dad and my children to pick the littered edge, looking for possibilities—some ugly, rusted-out, smelly, exquisite piece of junk that could be sanitized and transformed. I love a challenge and have partially furnished my house with possibility pieces from scrap piles, junkyards, garage sales, and family attics.

A municipal dump–raider has to be a possibility thinker: What can I possibly do with it? What can it become? Can I fix it? Who will help me? How?

Ask the Right Questions

These are questions one also asks of dump or junkyard events of life. Consider just one of the life situations that may have rendered your life to momentary junk, such as the ashes of your house, a faltering faith, a child born with a disability, infidelity of a spouse, a divorce or separation, or paralyzing guilt over a misspoken word or unintentional wound inflicted on a friend. There's no way a person can sit and look at one of the piles of junk in life without doing *something*. The question is, what will you do? Unfortunately, there is no formula such as removing the old paint, sanding, gluing, refinishing, or oiling. There's no single way to resurrect events from the scrap pile of life, but some principles have worked for me.

The first principle is *never reclaim a junk situation alone.* I need an awesome God who loves me and will go partners with me in reclamation. Only God can transform. All of us can work at it, and we must put sweat and prayer into any vision for it to become a reality, but how wonderful that we do not have to rebuild the broken relationship or event alone. With just enough dream left in us to move, God inspires us, gives us nudges and inclinations, and helps us become persons of vision who can transform.

Perspective, the second principle, requires me to ask myself if this junky event is really important enough to warrant all my excitement. A bundle of carved wood held together by rope and rescued from my grandma's garage moved with our family three times before I decided that it would, in fact, make a good kitchen table. The decision for life junk events, however, can't be delayed. So some perspective questions may help: Will time or the natural course of events heal it? Should I walk away from the situation because it is a brick wall instead of a bridge? The principle of perspective also reminds me that usually I don't have to deal with the entire garbage dump or junkyard all at once. At hand, just one junkyard event is at the top of the heap, so I just ask the possibility questions: What can I possibly do with it? What can it become? Can I fix it? Who will help me? How? I try to deal with one out-of-balance event at a time.

Pass it on!

If you are a reclamation person, remember that it is an intergenerational thing. You're a role model not only for family members but also for everyone around you. My father did more than take me to the dump. He had a few junkyard events of his own to contemplate. After coming to Kansas in a covered wagon, he was taken out of school at the age of ten and put to work making brick streets. He worked hard to overcome his lack of formal education. The 1929 depression, occurring after the death of his son, found him with two babies and a wife to feed and no job. He worked day-hire, doing every kind of labor, until perseverance and prayer got him reemployed by the railroad.

After thirty-five years with the railroad, he suddenly found his office locked along with the entire local Missouri, Kansas, and Texas shops and depot. Not old enough to retire, he did carpentry, finally becoming a contractor. His life junkyard events never got him down, because he faced them with courage and a walk with Jesus.

Reclamation

Some railroads still have what they call the Reclamation Plant, the place they take old wrecked or worn-out engines. In some plants workers reclaim or repair the old engines, while in other plants they simply take them apart, scrapping the bad equipment and saving the good for use on another engine. Deciding which is salvage and which is scrap is a little like triage at a hospital emergency room. My mother had her own form of triage. She blocked the door when we returned from the municipal dump and asked a pertinent question: "Where in the world do you think you're going to store that thing?"

But there is no triage in human life events. All persons and all events can be reclaimed, even those that seem as if they should go to the municipal dump, so hope is as important as perspective. Say, Yes, yes, yes! to fixing your scrap pile event. It can be reclaimed, and it can be reinvented. And the reinvented product may be bigger, better, more beautiful, more genuine than the original junk event.

Yes, I know people don't go to the municipal dump anymore, and it's illegal to burn garbage. But you know I'm not talking about that kind of reclamation. I'm talking about re-sorting, reclaiming, and reinventing. I'm talking about transformation of real, junkified life events into options for the future and doing it in the company of an awesome, loving God.

Related reading

The Bible is full of scrap pile events that are easy reading. Consider how Noah must have felt about the flood (Gen. 6:1—9:17). Although he followed God's directions, how would he have felt about seeing his land

and home go under water? about hearing the cries of his friends and seeing them drown?

The Old Testament book of Jonah is so short it can be read at night before falling asleep—but be careful about dreams. Jonah gets swallowed by a big fish. The story has layers of meaning that range from allegory and parable to a fictional story demonstrating exclusiveness.

Think about how Moses must have felt when he finally found a secure place with a family and property and God told him to go back and rescue the Hebrews from Egypt, and after all that he didn't even get to lead his people into the promised land. His junkyard events overlapped one another from the book of Exodus to parts of Numbers to Deuteronomy 34, where he views the promised land.

The apostle Paul took a junkyard event in which he was knocked flat by a blaze of light (Acts 9:1–31) and used it as a door opening to a new world of service for his Lord.

Escaping Perfection

For a long time my luck held. Jigsaw puzzles purchased at garage sales provided good, inexpensive entertainment. Spread on a smooth table with pieces sorted by colors and/or shapes and with edge pieces thrown to the middle for sorting, the picture materialized slowly. My favorite pictured a pretty little seaside village with shuttered, brightly painted houses nestled among the rocks with a variety of bleached, gray wooden boats beached next to the water. I worked on it until my eyes hurt. Ignoring household tasks and office mail, I became caught up in the challenge of getting it together. And I did. Almost.

There were four pieces missing: the head of a man walking on the beach, two border edges of water, and the corner of a fluffy cloud. The perfect rendition of the perfect English village of Clovelly had some eye-catching holes, making it hard to enjoy the scene. Again and again I searched the floor around my table for the missing pieces, but all I turned up were dust bunnies and a few Cheerios.

I have known only a few people who have had all the edge and center pieces in their lives formed into a perfect picture. There will be holes, or one of the straight-edged pieces that holds the picture together will disappear, and imperfection will be obvious. The picture-perfect person will eventually discover that it is hard, if not impossible, to be flawless. I know. I tried. Most people try.

How'd We Get That Way?

How did we get to the point where we think we have to be as perfect as a picture, all there and put together? Was it our first-grade writing teacher who demanded perfection? It became easier to strive for printed perfection than to stay in from recess to copy it over. Or was it our parents' fault? They made us make our bed over and over to make it neat, or they made us recut the grass to snip off the little stripes we had missed. They expected A's on report cards and S's in conduct. Maybe we wanted to be perfect—to beat out the competition in soccer, football, baseball, or chair tryouts in the school orchestra.

Could it be that we have been influenced by advertising? According to television, a teenager must have a *particular* brand of jeans, shoes, shirt, golf club, baseball bat, or roller blades in order to be acceptable. The fisherman and -woman with the largest catch, or the car that is a perfect match for a successful businessperson shows us a picture of how the commercial world wants us to present ourselves. We are easily influenced, often buying without thought of the statement we are making about ourselves—that is, that we want to be acceptable—and we translate that into "perfect."

On the job, we pretend that we make no mistakes. If work isn't finished on time, we carry it home in a briefcase, spending untold hours making it look right.

Some persons, however, spend time discovering the difference between doing their best job and expecting perfection both in themselves and others. Once they settle for simply doing their best, the burden of perfection is lifted, and they have the opportunity to be themselves. Freedom at last! No pretense, no pressure to live the perfect life.

Gayle found this new freedom the third time she became a mother. Exhausted with running the perfect home and searching for the perfect day care, one day she gave herself permission to be less than perfect. It was a turning point, a revelation that allowed her to reinvent her life. When she returned to work three months after the baby was born, she found—to her surprise—that she was not as demanding and critical of others, because she knew to the core of her being that others could not be perfect.

Surrendering the idea that we can in some way approach perfection requires rigorous honesty, and it isn't easy. Sometimes it is so painful we turn away, because the realization that we have had perfection as our goal for much of our lives has made us unbalanced, unhappy, and unfulfilled.

Perfection Exception

Could our striving to be perfect have its roots in sermons on perfection? Or did we read it in the Bible? It's hard to separate our rendition of the Bible from our personal interpretations of what it means to be perfect. Here are two examples.

Jesus teaches a crowd of people, instructing them to strive for perfection, and he tells them that love is the way to achieve it:

> Be perfect, therefore, as your heavenly Father is perfect (Mt. 5:48).

The apostle Paul is leaving his friends and gives them this good advice:

> Aim for perfection, listen to my appeal, be of one mind, live in peace. And the God of love and peace will be with you. (2 Cor. 13:11, NIV)

Jesus and Paul aren't telling us to be perfectionists in all that we do. They suggest imitating God's perfect love and loving ways. Our heavenly Father doesn't make a perfect cherry pie for a bake sale or spend a lot of time and money having perfect fingernails, the flawless barber cut, or the highest position in a company. God doesn't need the perfect car or have to keep the car litter- and dust-free. Nor does God keep a garage in spotless order, everything in its place and dusted once a week. Is that going on to perfection? "Be ye perfect" doesn't mean doing every chore in daily life perfectly or suffering pangs of guilt from the lack of perfection in every daily act.

Events that cause us to change our lifestyles present us with wonderful opportunities for learning something new. We are not and cannot become perfect. *We're free!* Free to turn loose of chains that have fooled us into thinking that we can be perfect. We can't spend all our time and energy trying to be the perfect employee, housekeeper, caregiver, parent, human being. Instead, we have an opportunity! More than an opportunity, it's a whole new attitude. Escape trying to be the perfect person. Strive only toward spiritual perfection. There's a big difference!

Phoenix with Flexibility

When a smashing event of great Change overtakes me, I sometimes picture myself as the fabled phoenix of Greek mythology. Storytellers agree that after living thousands of years, the phoenix would burn itself on a funeral pyre, and a new and beautiful phoenix would arise out of the ashes. The phoenix over the years has, for many people, become a symbol of immortality and rebirth. I have other Christian symbols of immortality and rebirth, but in a daily reinvention of life, the phoenix becomes a symbol for me to rise again from ashes.

With this in mind I often set out to conquer my world, making bold plans and designing just how I will enact them. This is what I call Plan A. Often, however, things don't go as planned, so I move to Plan B. Try as I may, even Plan B has pitfalls, so I revert to a plan I call Plan C: "Oh, Forget It."

Plan A

Plan A is enacted after careful consideration. It seems logical and expedient and is expected to be gratifying. It may not be perfect, but through imagery I have walked it in my mind, and it is my best map of accomplishment. Plan A is, as the name implies, carefully planned and filled with high expectations and desires.

An old Yiddish proverb says, "To make God laugh, make plans." I laughed when I heard it but then grew very serious, because I do not believe that God throws roadblocks into my plans. On the other hand, from God's viewpoint on time, a little laugh now and then might keep all of us from striving to keep Plan A at all costs. Unexpected events and limitations or inadequate planning may keep me from moving full speed ahead with Plan A. Instead of hand-wringing, a full assessment may lead me to jettison the plan and move to Plan B.

Plan B

Plan B is a modified Plan A, carried out late or on a lesser level. Expectations have to be lowered, and it may not be as logical or expedient as Plan A. Instead of the idealized version of the phoenix, Plan B runs along the lines of the nursery school story about the little engine that thought it could. The repetitious lines keep running through my head: "I think I can. I think I can. I think I can." Moving from Greek mythology as a symbol to a puffing little train going uphill lowers the classic quality of Plan B, but it is honorable and sometimes just the best a person can do.

Plan B can help fulfill obligations, and it can be rewarding. It's not really what I wanted to do, but it is the best at the moment. Here's an example from one of my friends:

On his way to make a very important speech, Jim feels prepared (Plan A) and enthusiastic. But wait! As he grabs the car keys to leave for City Hall where he will speak, the phone rings. "Marty did what?" he asks the caller. Glad to have the keys in his hand, Jim jumps into his car and heads for the hospital to consult with the orthopedic physician who will set Marty's leg. The news isn't good. After his consultation—but before the surgery that will be required to repair the knee—Jim inaugurates Plan B. He calls a coworker involved in his same cause with the request that he deliver the speech, but the willing coworker has a business conflict. After several calls, Jim finds no one who can deliver his speech. Plan B, which was Jim's partial solution to Plan A, is not working at all. Apprehensive, Jim sits in the hospital waiting room evaluating his options. Finally, he scribbles a note to the convener of the meeting, encloses it with his speech, hails a taxi, and pays the driver to deliver it to City Hall.

Oh, Forget It!

Jim has selected an option called Plan C: "Oh, Forget It." He has placed a priority on his son's well-being, and he has also acted responsibly by sending the speech. But he has completely abandoned Plan A and Plan B. Without knowing it, Jim has gone into Plan C. However, arriving at the hospital, he assesses the new situation and begins to formulate a Plan A to help him and his son meet this crisis.

Every day, all around us, people are caught in stressful events that make them scrap their plans. The example given was a series of events occurring in one day; however, they had long-term repercussions. At issue will be long-term care for Marty, promotion of the cause espoused in Jim's speech, and perhaps guilt over disappointing Jim's committee members, for whom he was to speak. While Jim's Plan C example seems simple, there are complex fingers of change that run in every direction, making it more difficult to choose between the three plans for coping—so, "Oh, forget it" is not as untroublesome as it seems, except in extreme cases calling for absolute surrender.

Absolute surrender has a valuable place and can be a lifesaver. Persons undergoing change events that make great demands on their time or energy or persons with health problems that are unpredictable can rest easy in the comfort of falling back on a Plan C. It is honorable. It should be guiltless. Plan C is based on wisdom. But it is very hard to declare, steeped as we are in loyalty and determination. Somehow, total surrender of Plans A and B seem easier if the surrender is labeled Plan C and practiced with honesty. Plan C says, "I gave it my best shot," or "I'm doing the best I can," or "I'm sorry, but this time I have to give it up."

Discouragement comes so easily when we are reinventing our lives that the easy way out would be to move to Plan C— "Oh, forget it!"—and get stuck there. Most people have good intentions and don't get stuck on "Oh, forget it!" but after time, Plan C might be such a handy way of operation that it could become a trap, and "Oh, forget it!" might leave some persons stuck in the ashes. So it is important to remember the phoenix.

After Plan C

Inside each of us is a core of creativity that can help us dream new dreams, celebrate life, envision a future, make plans that are logical and expedient, and rise again like the phoenix, shaking off the ashes of whatever burned us. Life may never be exactly the same after we have suffered losses. It may be accommodated, adjusted, or reinvented. Sometimes we can even use the ashes of what burned us as stepping stones to something new and useful.

Forget Shakespeare. What Is, Is!

Professional dramatist and poet William Shakespeare was a genius in characterization and plot, giving his characters speeches so masterfully crafted that they not only served the characters in pushing the play forward but also have passed into general usage. Bits and pieces have been quoted for more than 350 years by persons not even familiar with Shakespeare or his plays. The following are some of the more famous quotations:

The quality of mercy is not strain'd,
It droppeth as the gentle rain from heaven
Upon the place beneath.
  (*The Merchant of Venice*, Act IV, Sc. 1, 184–87)

How far that little candle throws his beams!
So shines a good deed in a naughty world.
  (*The Merchant of Venice*, Act V, Sc. 1, 90–91)

Neither a borrower, nor a lender be;
For loan oft loses both itself and friend,
And borrowing dulls the edge of husbandry.
  (*Hamlet*, Act I, Sc. 3, 75–77)

To be, or not to be: that is the question.
  (*Hamlet*, Act III, Sc. 1, 56)

This last quotation serves the actor well in Hamlet. However, when used as a question in life, it comes up short. Hamlet examines the choice of life versus death, an idea not entertained by most of us as an optional solution to a crisis situation, because what is, is. *The real question of life is, How will I handle what life has dealt me?*

Define Your Coping Skills

Skills for handling what life has dealt us vary with individuals. John may be passive, just waiting until something works out, turns up, or fades into the background. It works for him. Mary may be more aggressive, taking any road out of the rut she is in as long as she is in charge and the road is going somewhere. It works for her.

Define your own particular way of coping, either passive or aggressive or someplace in between, and you're on your way to saying, "Hey! It's all right to be this way." Such a statement carries with it the recognition that another person's way is all right for that person, too. Each can find a way to turn "what is" into something better that works for him or her.

There are many examples of turning "what is" into something better. Consider singer Marian Anderson, who began singing in the church choir when she was eight. By the age of twenty-two she was awarded a fellowship to study in Europe. Her rich voice made her a favorite all over Europe, and she sang for royalty. Returning to the United States, she received many accolades.

One of her greatest disappointments, however, occurred when a women's organization refused to let her sing in Washington's Constitution Hall because she was black. She chose to put a positive slant on "what was" by singing on the steps of Lincoln Memorial on Easter morning. Seventy-five thousand people came to show they did not support the racist stand taken by the women's organization. Later, Marian became the first black person chosen to sing regularly with the Metropolitan Opera Company. Marian Anderson worked aggressively around a wounding situation, turning it into triumph. She later received the Presidential Medal of Freedom and was elected into the Women's Hall of Fame.

Now consider Karl Loes, an atheist German political refugee befriended by a Lutheran pastor during World War II. Although Karl was unable to really understand the pastor's willingness to share Jesus with him or to understand at the time the stories of Jesus, he accepted the minister's hospitality as a matter of course and eventually drifted away into the underground of Nazi Germany.

Two years later, when the pastor helped clear out a cellar where the Nazis had executed several prisoners, he found that Karl Loes had been held prisoner and before his death had written the following words on the cellar wall:

I believe in the sun when it is not shining;
I believe in love when I do not feel it;
I believe in my Lord Jesus even when he is silent.

These words from a dark cellar are printed on posters around the world today, giving hope and encouragement to persons whose faith has been challenged. Karl Loes, a man who accepted his situation and decided what to do about it, never preached a sermon, left no books or pictures, and is famous for nothing else, but in the midst of evil he slowly allowed a new faith to enter his life.

Now consider the Reverend Harold H. Wilke, pastor, teacher, writer, and advocate for people with disabilities. He was born without arms. In answer to the question, How will I handle what has been dealt me? he worked to become ordained as a minister of The United Church of Christ. "He has had a distinguished career in four areas of service: the Church, rehabilitation medicine, teaching and government...He currently directs the Healing Community which promotes awareness about access to a life of faith...and is a founding director of the National Organization on Disability."[3] He has lived a full and loving life without arms and accepted with his foot a pen President George Bush used in signing the 1990 Americans with Disabilities Act.

When actor Christopher Reeves was thrown from a horse in 1995, he became paralyzed. With great courage he has worked to become weaned from the respirator for longer periods of time, and he spends hours a day in physical therapy. The remaining time he divides between family, creative pursuits in movie making and acting, and political pursuits. He accommodated to what was dealt him, but came out fighting for spinal cord research through advocacy and fund-raising. Many persons will benefit because of his spirit and his advocacy work. Other stories illustrating great decisions to work with "what is" can be found in any current newspaper or magazine. They are the positive stories we so often overlook, hidden as they are under bad news headlines.

Boldness Called For

The "what is, is" philosophy is not meant to be "Pollyanna," a giving in to conditions or events that twist a life. Rather, it signifies accepting events that cannot be changed *at the moment* and boldly making something satisfying with the life that is left.

God enables us, each in our own coping style, to move on into the future as a being blessed. Without arms, paralyzed, or facing death or prejudice, we can choose wisely what we will do with what has been dealt into our lives. We really can make a bold choice to reinvent.

Detours to Everywhere
(*or:* Trouble on the Interstate)

The Jura Mountain Range forms part of the boundary between Switzerland and France. Sheer rock walls of the Jura Gorge reach thousands of feet up on each side of the highway with a beauty so spectacular that Bob and I hardly noticed the dozen or so triangular road signs reading "Umleitung!" They were persistent, and as the road got rough, I frantically searched the English-German dictionary for the word, but couldn't find it. We began to worry. As the concrete road got narrow and turned to gravel, we found ourselves shifted into a winding, narrow, throw-rocks-at-the-windshield detour, and we discovered that *Umleitung* means "get ready for a traffic shift."

We made it through the pass without falling into the river or sliding off the road, but as we drove along slowly, making stops and starts, we talked about detours in life that kept us from moving full speed ahead to our goals or objectives. Except for oohing and aahing over the lovely mountain scenery, we spent the rest of the afternoon recounting detours in life that we had taken.

So, What's a Detour?

A detour may mean that road work or a life event will keep you from moving full speed ahead. In a detour, momentum is stopped; you may have to change lanes and follow strange arrows, you may have to take a different route, or you may end up at another destination. A detour may mean you have to forget to hurry; slow down and be extremely cautious and resourceful as you pause your fast-forward motion or trudge toward your goal.

Detours also bring surprises. Notice that when you take a detour, the road often takes you to a little cove, a village, a special place you would otherwise have missed. Life also is like that. Many detours have driven us to invent new careers, to find new friends or better ways of doing things.

Such detours and their outcomes are learning experiences that teach us that detour is life itself, not time out from forward movement. All lives zigzag. That is, no life goes in a straight line toward a goal, and the person who learns to love the questions of life and to love the challenge of exploring new ways and answers can really relax and enjoy life.

Yes, I do know that some detours are meaningless delays! They cause us to sit in life's traffic and burn gasoline and breathe other people's fumes. Other detours just try our patience and take away what we have earned by hard work or by attempts at being Christian. While sitting in the detour traffic of life, it's a good idea to remember that *God is present in all detours, even if we're disappointed that God didn't fix the road.*

Trouble on the Interstate

You're not alone in trouble on the interstate and unexpected detours. Danny and Angela, young working lawyers, have just built a new house and are expecting a baby. Angela plans to take leave and then return to work when the baby is three months old. The beautiful red-headed girl with big blue eyes arrives on schedule, but she is born with a hole in her heart. Angela needs to stay home full-time to care for the baby, but medical bills mount. Danny and Angela sell their dream home and move to a less expensive neighborhood, as their child's illness requires them to change their lifestyle and the way they spend their money.

Nancy's spouse betrays her. Suddenly, she trusts no one. In front of her loom several roads, and all of them beckon at once. Her sense of who she is and what she wants seems to have vanished. Divorce has left her without confidence or money. Her plan for a happy family life with children is gone. She must choose an alternate route.

Bill's best friend dies unexpectedly. Grief slows him down as he tries to face the reality of his friend's death and the renewed awareness that he, too, will one day die. The detour of grief makes him rethink the direction of his life.

Bobbie enjoys her Sunday school class and the worship service at her church. But lately she has been hearing ideas in Sunday school that don't fit her system of beliefs. She is upset to the point that she has trouble sleeping, and she finds herself caught in a cycle of worry and indecision. Having her religious beliefs challenged is very painful. Hasn't she spent years putting together her belief system? She has to take time out to investigate where she got her ideas and what the Bible says. She grows from the experience, but for a while it seems to be a diversion from her forward motion in life. The detour causes her pain, self-doubt, and time, but investigation is enlightening. Looking back, she will say that it was the beginning of opening her heart and mind to God for growth.

Some Ultimate Detours

God told Abraham to go to a faraway land. He said okay. Who had to do the packing? Sarah! She had to bundle up their entire household, pots and pans, skins, pottery, lamps, tents, livestock, and servants and follow Abraham wherever God told him to go. Talk about detours! Sarah couldn't just open a Bible and enjoy the colored maps at the back to see where they had been and where they were going. This faithful wife just went.

Sarah was barren for years and years, so her dreams of her own children were laid to rest until she was ninety years old and found herself pregnant. Now I ask you, who wants night nursing at the age of ninety? That may be the ultimate detour. Abraham, the father now over one hundred years old, laughed himself silly when the angel told him he would be a father. But it happened. The Bible doesn't tell us if he helped with the night feedings.

And what about Moses? His whole life was one big detour, from being hidden in the river and raised in a different culture to escaping into distant mountains. When he heard God and saw the burning bush, he had to go back, exit, come back, lay back. That poor guy could never go full speed ahead to reach his destination. The destination kept changing, and his speed was variable, even after God sent the commandments. And he had to sit in traffic and breathe other people's fumes instead of going into the promised land.

What about the wise men who followed a star to find the small Jesus? Who gave them a road map? The star was leading them, but then, *Umleitung!* Herod got in the act. After they visited Jesus, they took a huge detour, going back home without a star to guide them and on unfamiliar ground, all in order to avoid Herod. It was a gift to Jesus. *The wise men made their detour count.*

Danny and Angela, Bill, Bobbie, Sarah and Abraham, Moses, and the wise men reframed their detours and reinvented their goals and visions, allowing challenging events to become positive lessons.

Learn to Reframe

One of the most valuable lessons I have learned about detours came from reading Paul's letter to the Philippians. His good advice taught me to reframe a detour, that is, to hold it up and twist it around and look at it in a different light by looking for a blessing in it. Even sadness and trial bring the knowledge that we can celebrate God's presence in our lives, and halting places and extra stop signs can give us time to rely on God to show us a new path or roadway.

> Rejoice in the Lord always; again I will say, Rejoice. Let your gentleness be known to everyone. The Lord is near. Do not worry about anything, but in everything by prayer and supplication with thanksgiving let your requests be made known to God. And the peace of God, which surpasses all understanding, will guard your hearts and your minds in Christ Jesus. (Phil. 4:4–7)

What are we supposed to think about while on detour? I call those things the whatevers, the positive thoughts that help bring peace of mind and heart.

> Finally, beloved, whatever is true, whatever is honorable, whatever is just, whatever is pure, whatever is pleasing, whatever is commendable, if there is any excellence and if there is anything worthy of praise, think about these things. Keep on doing the things that you have learned and received and heard and seen in me, and the God of peace will be with you. (Phil. 4:8–9)

And One More Thing

Positive thoughts while on detour are important, but questions are paramount. Questions that help reframe the detour need thought and time. Thought, because we should not merely pass off the detour as ordinary and because the questions may change as the detour event becomes integrated into daily life. Time, because the experiences that drive us to new discoveries and answers take time. Without bold questions and time spent seeking and thinking about them, we receive few answers.

Mace, Mobilenet, and the Extra Edge

Don't you love movies in which an evil vampire is menacing a fair young maiden, and she suddenly holds up a cross from which light dazzles the vampire, and he slinks away? What a wonderful magic zap!

Personally, I'd like to have a cross like that. So would a lot of good Christian people who have been mugged, almost murdered, just plain sick to death, or down and out and living under a bridge. Since fiction is fiction and I don't have such a cross, I began to wonder, "What, if any, extra edge do Christians have to help keep them safe?"

In the field of personal safety, commonsense precautions come to mind, such as parking near lights, locking all doors, carrying mace, wearing a money belt, traveling in pairs, carrying a mobile phone, having a weapon handy, carrying a loud alarm, not wearing jewelry to the grocery store or ATM, and staying alert.

Then, in the health field, precautions include eating broccoli, keeping fattening food beyond fingertip reach, inhaling at the health food store, taking vitamins, hiring a local herbalist, visiting a dentist at least once a year, and so on.

Beyond common sense, what edge does a Christian person have that will help him or her survive a crisis? After not smoking, a person gets lung cancer. During chemotherapy for one disease, the chemicals cause another. Persons in some religious groups who wear special blessed clothing are sometimes personally assaulted. So, what can a person count on? Does a Christian really have an edge?

The Edge

Yes, a Christian has an edge that allows him or her to meet daunting or even terrifying circumstances with a certain measure of assurance. People everywhere will relate exciting, mysterious, and inspiring "from the edge" stories that are testimonies to unusual events and unusual faith. These are authentic, believable. But what about us ordinaries who have no clue about how to dazzle a vampire with a cross?

One way to keep an edge for panic events is to avoid famine of the soul. For this edge, one has to plan ahead, so start planning. A close walk with God puts you in tune with God's wishes for your life. Then, when panic or danger sets in, the most natural thing in the world is turning your heart to God. It's not actually holding a cross up to ward off trouble or evil, but holding an internal cross or light to register holy ideas.

Every situation has its own special need, whether it's a custody battle, a carjacking or mugging, or a terrifying medical diagnosis. Asking for specific help without telling God what to do affords a much better "edge" than just yelling "Help! Help!" to anyone in general. A close walk with God—including prayer, meditation, and networking with others who also walk with God—shores up the soul.

Another way to have an edge during panic events is to live in the richness of God's Word, found in the Bible. This is avoiding famine of the Word. It means to familiarize, seek to understand, memorize, recite, and look for new meanings in scripture. When we ignore the Bible and don't take time to integrate it into our lives, we lose the edge when a sudden event is thrust upon us.

Memorizing verses from the Bible can be a godsend, often giving us a lifeline. If you or your loved one were locked in the trunk of a murderer's car, or a best friend had betrayed you, what would you do? Recite "Now I lay me down to sleep" one hundred times? Or would it be more comforting to fall back to bits of scripture? Perhaps you might say,

> The LORD is my shepherd, I shall not want.
>> He makes me lie down in green pastures;
> he leads me beside still waters;
>> he restores my soul. (Ps. 23:1–3a)

You might say,

> But you, O LORD, are a shield around me. (Ps. 3:3a)

You might recite this instead of "Now I lay me down to sleep":

> The LORD is my light and my salvation;
>> whom shall I fear?
> The LORD is the stronghold of my life;
>> of whom shall I be afraid? (Ps. 27:1)

You might recall the story from Mark 6:45–56 in which Jesus, walking along the shore, notices the disciples in their boat straining at the oars against a heavy wind. He walks out to them, nearly frightening them to death, tells them who he is, and tells them to take courage and not be afraid. Then he climbs into the boat with them, and the wind dies down. That's what Jesus does for us: He climbs into the boat and helps us calm the storms.

Scripture bits certainly aren't magic, so perhaps remembering the essence of familiar biblical stories can help the mind and heart hang to the edge of the tragedies or events that unsettle us. A good example of such events can be found in a story of the disciples. Oh, how they grieve when Jesus dies, their grief perhaps tinged with guilt that they went to sleep when he asked them to watch with him in Gethsemane. Yet they are thrilled to see him again and reinvent their lives without him, carrying out ideals of the way he lived his life and passing on what he taught them. Peter, who is immersed in the special guilt of denying that he even knew Jesus, goes on to be a rock in the new work of "Christian church."

Certainly, if the Bible had a subtitle, it might read, "The Story of Life-Changing Events and Mistakes," for the stories of betrayal, suspicion, murder, death, resurrection, joy, and messages for life are there. It's never too late to look to these stories for clues in the events of life. Avoid famine of the soul and live in the richness of God's Word, carry mace and your mobile phone, and you really will have an edge.

2

Reinventing
SELF

Almost without our knowledge, events of change begin to define who we are. What has been required of us may make self-esteem suffer and body image change so that we are strangers to ourselves. At this time it is imperative to stand firmly on an internal stepping-stone while asking honest questions and looking for lasting answers. But we must assume that other forms of change will continue in our lives, and we will have the wonderful opportunity of redefining ourselves again and again. It sounds formidable, but it can also be an exciting adventure!

No one can really start over with a whole new self, so perhaps "reinventing self" is a misnomer. To find out who we really are, we must become possibility thinkers and learn to scrutinize ourselves, widening our horizons as we redefine ourselves. God can help us realize our potential, and often when the adjustments are made, we discover that we really aren't our old selves any longer. We have had a rebirth. That's awesome!

Do Mirrors Lie?

A recent television commercial showed a monkey looking at himself in the mirror. Below the picture was a written caption: When a monkey looks at himself in the mirror, does he know he's a monkey?

That day I looked in the mirror and thoughtfully asked my reflection, "Who are you? Do you know who you are?" I had spent a lifetime knowing myself and shaping who I was. Suddenly, in a moment of truth, I was a different person. I looked fine with my new haircut and makeup on just right. But inside I felt like a squashed cantaloupe. I was physically ill. Yet there was that put-together person in the mirror. Do mirrors lie? Yes, but they are just glass, and what they reflect is open to truthful recognition or interpretation.

Mirrors are, however, important. Remember the times you held a baby to a mirror? Amid giggles and patty-cakes, you'd ask, "See the pretty baby?" Babies are aided in their sense of identity from seeing their reflections. A young child runs to a mirror to see the gap left by the tooth he has just pulled, and a young ballerina student practices her pirouettes in front of a full-length mirror.

Teenagers spend hours in front of mirrors, moaning over bodies that look out of kilter—perhaps a short leg, ears that are too big, or a nose that's too little. During the teen years, even the reflection of a broken fingernail can become a major event. The mirror becomes at the same time their best friend of reassurance and their enemy when they see themselves in a biased way.

Middle-aged persons run to the mirror when the hair starts to fall out or turn gray or when wrinkles grace the chin line. Actors use makeup mirrors and can't become their characters without them. Persons with neurological impairments look in the mirror to reaffirm parts of their bodies they can't feel.

Mirrors can be reassuring, and they do influence the images we have of our bodies. They help us define boundaries for ourselves and aid us in presenting to the world a better image. But the person we see is not who we are. We *are* a sum total of many ideas and heartbeats. Understanding who we are is a lifetime project of adventure and discovery, a project that makes us ask, "Who is that person inside my skin?" and "Who tells me who I am?"

Do Others Define Us?

Other people and things help us define ourselves. We are someone's child. We are someone's mother or father. An illness may imply that we are an illness-person. An adult child's divorce may split our loyalties, rob us of grandchildren, and tear us into two parts. In the end, we may feel that someone's divorce defines us. The church may so consume our time and effort that it comes to define us. Money and getting it may define us. An abusing spouse may want to define us as evil, always wrong, or stupid, overpowering our own sense of who we are. Or someone in our workforce may constantly threaten us until we mold our thinking into a certain way. We may see a picture in our heads as a definition of ourselves. Others may influence us, but if we allow others to actually define who we are, after a while our concept of self can become blurred, and we may end up play-acting life, trying to act out an integrated picture of what we think other persons expect of us.

Do Events Define Us?

Some events scramble our lives, challenge our theology, and push life into fast-forward: A parent is ill, a child dies, we are fired from our job, the church disappoints us, a hurricane takes our house, we are diagnosed with an incurable disease, we win the lottery, terrorism makes us feel unsafe, or by what seems to be a miraculous act, we are saved from the jaws of death. Other events that cannot be reversed, such as stealing or adultery, give us the message that we have ruined our lives. If accepted, this message can, in fact, come to define us, making life seem hopeless and giving us false messages about ourselves. A diagnosis of chronic illness may so consume our time and energy that we may begin to feel that we have lost our personality, and the event of illness defines us. We may come to imagine that these and other events tell us who we are. Although they do not *tell* us who we are, they may cause us to *redefine* who we are. We are changed, never again the same.

Although other people and everyday events do influence the self-pictures we carry inside our heads, they do not define who we are. We can and must accept the responsibility for discovering or rediscovering who we are. Seeking truth, we ask the question, "Who is that person inside my skin?"

Love Lavished

Under our skin is someone made in the image of God. A spiritual being! Again and again the Bible says that man and woman are created in God's own image, a spiritual one. And the Bible also tells us that we are God's children.

> See what love the Father has given us, that we should be called children of God. (1 Jn. 3:1a)

> You are children of the LORD your God. You must not lacerate yourselves or shave your forelocks for the dead. For you are a people holy to the LORD your God; it is you the LORD has chosen out of all the peoples on earth to be his people, his treasured possession. (Deut. 14:1–2)

To paraphrase, this says, "You're children of God. Don't do pagan acts. You belong to God." Any event or act that makes you turn away from God might be considered pagan. Valuing money or job or recognition more than God might be considered pagan. The Bible can be a guide to daily living that interprets the opposite of *pagan,* which is *Godly behavior.*

With the understanding that we are loved by God, made in the image of God, and are children of God, we can feel secure yet free in looking under our skin to discover who we really are. Where and how do we begin? Everyone learns to define *self* in different ways, so you may make a conscious effort that is very workable. Here are some things that continue to work for me.

1. *Undertake* this like any new beginning by asking that God take this journey with you, and along the way remember that you can talk to the companion who is walking the journey with you. It's not a one-time request; it's a "walk with me always" prayer.

2. *Try to reverse* hectic stress events that consume time and keep a false focus on life. Begin by relaxing alone. Do something you like to do. Just for you and no one else. Drink coffee on the patio and enjoy the birds, go jogging, do your nails, read a poem, hit a tennis ball against a wall, play the piano or another musical instrument, sketch a picture, keep a journal. Or perhaps your enjoyment comes from running four miles or paddling a canoe. Ask yourself, How long did it take me to get outside the stress box and decide what to do? and What did I learn about my state of mind from doing this?

3. *Learn to look* into the face of truth. It takes courage. Ask God for help with recognizing areas of your life you are reluctant to look into because they are dark. It is important to discover parts of yourself that you don't like, learn from them, and keep them from becoming haunting ghosts. Acknowledging mistakes and unhealthy desires is a step toward seeking forgiveness, which enables you to get rid of the haunting ghosts. It may be easier to forgive others than to forgive yourself, but take the time to do it! Honesty also allows you the privilege of losing modesty and humility while you look at goodness and virtue in yourself. After peeling the banana of your life, the discovery of unnoticed gems of wisdom and good habits and previously made correct decisions may cause you to celebrate.

4. *Learn to cherish* your history and affirm your past. Even grim events from the past can teach valuable lessons for the future. Once you don't allow events to actually define who you are, their importance becomes smaller and your perspective changes,

making it possible to affirm and cherish them as part of your history.

5. *Celebrate* who you have been and who you are. Spend time looking back at events in life that have provided joy and satisfaction. Everyone can recall scenes that vibrate with color and beauty. Replaying them often keeps attitude in perspective. If your stress event involves a person who repeatedly blackens the scenes with grief, remember that time may help the situation. However, this situation may need professional help. Seeking professional help can be a way of celebrating your life without letting a person or event dictate who you are. The person or event becomes less powerful.

6. *Find* a prayer partner or group that will assist you in the quest to find out who you really are. Some events and persons in our lives are so shocking that we are numb and may seem at the moment unable to pray. Confidence in the prayer of others is powerful and soothing.

7. *Remind* yourself that life is a pilgrimage and that the adventure of redefining yourself is a lifetime project; however, your life isn't engraved in stone, and you get one, then two, then three, and then unlimited opportunities to reinvent yourself. You are becoming! Now, that's good news!

> Deep inside my skin
> where the light of God shines
> is a person
> created by God
> in God's spiritual image.

> Rediscovery of this person
> can be like untangling beautiful,
> colored yarn.
> Nothing is lost.
> Even the red and purple knots and tangles
> are beautiful.

Events and people may help mold our personalities, but it is up to us to take responsibility for who we are. The next time you look in a mirror, smile and say, "Hey, you beautiful yarn, you *are*, and you are also *becoming*."

Who Am I?
(One Short Leg or a Broken Fingernail)

Finally, the magazine came in the noon mail. Eagerly, I opened *Accent on Living* to the article I had written, "How to Buy a Wheelchair." Written with humor, I considered it snappy and upbeat, but as I read, there were transparent moments when I knew that body image had come to the front burner of my life. The way I looked to myself and to others had changed. Not only was I sporting a new red and black wheelchair, my fingernails kept getting snagged on the wheel spokes. When adapting to new images, even the most minute detail is magnified. I often think in cartoonlike pictures, so I had an image in my head of myself sitting in the wheelchair at a meeting, and all eyes were on my large hands with huge, snagged fingernails.

Delving into research literature, I discovered body image to include more than the way I looked to myself and to others. For many, including myself, perceptual image is dependent on visual and tactile experience and on information from within the body. For example, I am not always certain where some parts of my body are. My body is giving me signals that aren't reliable when part of my face is numb or when my hands do not have the familiar feelings that help me hold on to a cup or glass. For me, these feelings, or the lack of them, sometimes give me an image of myself as a klutz. I still joke about being a klutz, but I know that this numbness and consequent clumsiness don't define me. For other persons with disabilities, such as those who are paraplegic or quadriplegic or persons with amputated limbs, the body image is more critical when false data seems to arise from a false limb or when perceived space is not there.

The distortions of size, shape, extension, and space or non-space are medical problems to be dealt with on an individual basis. My particular interest narrowed to the practical application of body image and how a person with an altered body image needs to understand the stages of adapting to change in this image.

Keeping things in perspective becomes very important when we realize that changes in body image are in force when one or more life-changing event occurs. Any cataclysmic Change seems to cause self-absorption; for the moment, we think we are the center of the universe, and, truly, our universe is out of balance.

"Self-esteem, identity, behavior, personality, and self-concept are closely intertwined with one's concept of body image," Ilene Morof Lubkin says in *Chronic Illness Impact and Interventions.*[4] It's easy to see that any or all of these may be distorted if we fail to accept and adapt to the changes in our bodies caused by chronic illness or other impairment. The perceived body image of visible impairments or illnesses seems very prominent, but persons with visually undetectable body changes often suffer the most. Joint replacement or installation of a heart valve or pacemaker requires adjustment time. Mastectomies, prostate surgery, a new inside-the-ear hearing aid, a new, perfectly fitted and ocularist-designed eyeball not visible to the casual observer—these require adaptation and redefinition of body image.

In my case, moving from a walking aid to buying a wheelchair was a very liberating experience, because now I can be more independent and move with less pain. On the flip side, I have to understand the stages of adapting to change in order to remain productive and creative. From research, I learned that persons who understand that there are typical stages of handling illness tend to be more patient with themselves and don't feel as if they are "cracking up" or "not living up to my faith or my better self." Knowledge of these stages is like a permission slip that says, "Take your time, but know that you will get through this." Understanding these stages often allows a person to conclude, "God is with me in every stage."

Caregivers, once knowledgeable of the adapting stages, can give appropriate assistance at each stage and can patiently chart the progress of their loved ones. The ability or inability to adjust to bodily changes and self-perception is influenced by family, social group, church, and a person's own self-image and theological focus.

The term *stages* may seem misleading. Persons usually move in progression along a line of recovery and may expect the next step toward regaining balance in life to be a certain way. As you know, life zigzags, going up and down and around the next bend, and cannot be charted on a list with numbers. However, for convenience in understanding, I am using the term *stages.*

Stages of Adapting to Change

THE FIRST STAGE of adapting to Change is *admission* that something is wrong. No matter how hard we try, the symptom or change event does not go away. For many persons, especially those in denial about their lack of perfection or those whose religious beliefs indicate sickness or other calamity as a punishment from God, facing these things as a real possibility is daunting. Looking an illness or disability squarely in the face takes courage, and it seems easier if family and friends encourage rather than criticize.

THE SECOND STAGE is the *impact of illness* on the body. A person's time, energy, and money go into coping with the disability itself. Trips to the doctor or hospital for testing consume time. Pain, the fight for survival, adapting to side effects of medication, and treatments all require coping. During this phase we wonder, *Why me?* Wishing for a different or more correct diagnosis, we may seek a second, third, or fourth opinion or may feel pressured to do so by a family member. We may feel victimized or angry with ourselves. For some persons, denial allows time to hold the self together and absorb the impact of the illness.

THE THIRD STAGE, *retreat,* is natural as the ill person becomes aware of the bodily changes that have occurred and begins to discover that life changes are called for. It may become apparent that the condition is more than a fancy inconvenience; life may never be the same. Some diseases cause denial of part of the body when the brain actually does not acknowledge an arm, leg, or side of the body. Other diseases cause numbness or uncontrollable movement of body parts, and an eye may not be felt or a foot is absent for a time.

Some chronically ill persons have invisible illnesses in which the body parts are all there, but they will not function in the manner to which they have been accustomed. For example, a patient with a heart condition may learn that the body cannot be relied on to go up stairs or run a marathon. A patient with cancer may have part of the body removed, so the body is no longer familiar. Children with birth defects and/or those born with missing limbs who later receive artificial replacements also go through a struggle with body image. A person with a hearing aid may feel acutely aware that his or her ear is the largest part of the body and think that everyone is seeing that hearing aid as a huge apparatus. Sometimes a cane user will feel that the cane is part of his body. A nonspeaking person who uses an electrical box for sound may feel as if that sound is a product of his body; it is part of him.

At various times in life a new moment of revelation of the disability's meaning may cause regression. For example, a child with growth hormone problems may not mind being small until middle school days when his peers outgrow him, or a woman may discover, while trying to conceive, that she cannot bear children. Retreat time is required for a person to begin to take it all in. This becomes a time for *resting and regrouping* as the person gets acquainted with a new body image. ("It's my self, but not my self. So who is my self?

IN THE FOURTH STAGE, *reality and losses are faced.* Real or distorted body changes make us seek truth. Waking up to the facts of a change in body image usually is a mourning procedure. Facing "who myself really is" can be a time of sad discovery. For example, a hiker with a permanent foot problem can no longer see him- or herself with the label "hiker." Limitations are assessed. Grief is acknowledged. Anger is recognized and may be dealt with. Many persons work through grief and anger to new affirmations of their real selves as spiritual, without discounting body loss. At this point an individual may choose to remain an illness-person, a victim, or become a person-person.

DURING THE FIFTH STAGE, a period of *reconstruction* can begin. After learning about disease progressions and physical possibilities, the head and heart can take on reconstruction suitable for each illness. Reconstruction can begin when even a small sense of balance is returned to daily life, when we either allow or force ourselves to work, play, think, and act like a person rather than an illness.[5]

It's myself but not myself. So it's a modified self, but still a person with a name, gifts to share, fun to seek, joy to express, sorrow to express, a book to read, a job to do, and so forth. The hiker may become a sitting bird watcher. A person with a hearing impairment may in turn be thankful for the small apparatus that lets her hear her grandchildren laugh.

Body image is tied in with all of a person's life, so reconstruction can burst brilliantly or grow slowly as experiences, inner resources, and support systems enter our lives. During this time, new perspectives on life appear or new talents may be discovered. Happy discovery can occur. For example, a librarian may become a stay-at-home writer. A new attitude can change the future. Sometimes the new attitude begins with the realization that life must be reinvented every day as we understand and live with the requirements of an illness. Here is great challenge! But here is great opportunity!

THE SIXTH STAGE may be like *a seesaw.* Adjustment and reconstruction of body image is not a one-time event. Setbacks, digressions from new disease, and regressions of old disease require constant retreat, acknowledgment, and reconstruction. Setbacks are often the most depressing and discouraging times, and it is normal to revert to the first or other stages of understanding the impact of the illness. Setbacks are likely to cause pity parties, because the hard road ahead is known. On the other hand, because the road is known, it is easier to hope, easier to work toward a new direction. The seesaw stage is really a mixed bag of tricks.

By now, if you aren't ill and have studied through these stages, you have already figured it out. All Change events are marked by these same stages or areas of emotional work.

After a while, some people say, reinvention of life gets easier because of self-confidence gained from previous experiences. However, a balanced life as a person-person, as opposed to an illness-person or other Change-person, is not free. An investment of patience and prayer and time is required, but the efforts yield great reward.

The Cornfield

I'm from Kansas. I watched Grandpa Wikle plant corn, cultivate it, and lay it by. I grew up watching corn grow tall and green, observing its tassels, checking the maturity of the kernels. I wanted it in a hurry, ready for the boiling pot, then on the table with melted butter and salt. I was amazed that Grandpa didn't stand out there in the cornfields every day telling it to grow faster. However, year after year it was the same: A certain rhythm of growth was expected by Grandpa. He trusted this rhythm. When tended crops grew to a certain stage and cultivators couldn't hoe out weeds and aerate the soil, the crop was laid-by to mature. Grandpa rested, went fishing, or did animal swapping. Sometimes he fixed the barn or a fence.

Years earlier, when Grandpa moved from operating a restaurant in Erie, Kansas, to farming, he somehow learned the patience and rhythm of life and farming, which sustained him until his death at the age of ninety-three.

Part of the rhythm of growing things, he had learned, was the laying-by, a time for quiet growth. I didn't know I had learned this until a bad experience of rejection hit me, and only laying-by time and patience helped me regain balance in my life.

When an event or an illness stops us in our tracks, the rhythm and balance of life feels like a broken teeter-totter. Frantic hand-wringing doesn't help, and we have to wait for the idea of how we "are" to sink in with a new perspective. During this vulnerable time honesty is hard to come by, for we may be working with uncomputed facts and incomplete information, or we may be caught in avoidance and denial. Resting time is needed.

THE LAYING-BY

When life reaches a certain pitch
From which
There is no retreat, yet no looking forward,
It makes you wonder where to run.
Where do you go with no energy?
Where do you go when beliefs feel jaded?
Where do you take pain when trust is broken?
Where is the blueprint for an uncertain future?
Run to the cornfields and hide among the stalks.
Be still.

Watch the patient farmer trustingly stop plowing and
weeding
While he waits for growth.
It's the "laying-by."

Inside a shady, cool row of green
Suspend life at a resting pace.
Ease in God's calm inner fields.
Just be. And wait, perhaps, for growth.
perhaps for courage
perhaps for self awareness
perhaps for God awareness.
Just be still.[6]

The act of being still is active. To be still means to hush up. It means to quit fretting, scheming, blaming, and figuring on forward motion for tomorrow. This positive act of hushing up is one of the requirements for getting to know the person you are reinventing.

Be still, and know that I am God! (Ps. 46:10)

Soaring

Have you met any victims lately? You see them on television every day—the kid in a wheelchair who was hit by a drunk driver, the company employee whose skin has been damaged by chemical burns, the kidnapped baby, the elder person who was cheated out of a life's savings, a person of any age overtaken by disease. Being a victim is unfair. Anger, grief, disgust, and denial are often the first reactions. They are legitimate feelings that must be worked through.

I'd feel like a victim, and I'd *be* a victim, if someone whacked me in the head and took my purse. As a victim I'd be angry and disgusted, too. However, what happens to the body and soul if I *stay* mad and remain a victim is a matter of record. Things such as high blood pressure, skin eruptions, and onset of a sore throat or worse things have been documented by doctors and psychologists as reactions to prolonged anger. For this and other reasons, forgiveness is crucial to a healing process that allows one to soar.

Dr. Carol A. Kelleher, clinical consultant for Associated Catholic Charities, says that it is important to remember that forgiveness is an intellectual decision that is separate from one's emotions. "Forgiveness is a spiritual and psychological process," Kelleher says. Only when the mind makes the conscious decision to forgive can the heart follow. When this happens, forgiveness becomes a life-giving process, using the message of love.[7] A sense of release to move forward comes only when the *decision* is made.

Only then can the process of forgiveness begin. It's not instantaneous.

The challenge of moving from victim to manager of a reinvented life is a personal choice anyone can make. It calls for possibility thinking in many areas of life from employment to family and community life. One has to ask honest but creative questions: What are my options now? Do I have to do this alone? Who will help me? What talents lie undiscovered inside me? What is my most important goal for *right now*? For later? It's time to be bold, think big, think future. It's time to think *soar*!

Soaring requires the desire to soar and the willingness to look away from victim actions and pictures and, often in a spirit of deliberate forgiveness, to look at life as many celebrations. No ostrich-head-in-the-sand stuff, just glimpses of good, a way of expecting something good, and, when it happens, a willingness to let yourself go and say, "Whoopee! Thank you, God."

Soar in Good Company

While sitting on a glacier in Canada one summer, I saw two huge birds flying tandem. Although their wing tips weren't touching, they seemed to be a unit, a pair soaring in the wind so close in formation they were one. Over and around me they soared. I thought of God soaring with me, paired with me.

Soaring is not quite like flying. Of course, I know I can't literally fly without an airplane. I tried once when I was seven. My friend Betty and I jumped off the stilted doghouse into a pile of leaves. That first lesson brought me a sprained ankle. And although my power chair moves fast, I have accepted the fact that I can't run, but I can have a walk in faith and surges of joy. Music helps me put optimism on the front burner. Who can hear the horn solo from *Romeo and Juliet* or the string section soaring to great heights in *A Midsummer Night's Dream* without feeling surges of joy?

Soaring is a matter of getting in touch with inner strength. Soaring is a matter of the heart and spirit. It is yellow sunbursts, stripes of purple fading into red. It's rainbows in the head. It's joy in knowing. It's warm feeling. It's triumph of a sort that makes a person feel thirty feet tall. The Bible encourages us to believe that we can have these feelings.

> Do you not know?
>> Have you not heard?
> The LORD is the everlasting God,
>> the Creator of the ends of the earth.
> He will not grow tired or weary,
>> and his understanding no one can fathom.
> He gives strength to the weary,
>> and increases the power of the weak.
> Even youths grow tired and weary,
>> and the young men stumble and fall;
> but those who hope in the LORD
>> will renew their strength.
> They will soar on wings like eagles;
>> they will run and not grow weary,
>> they will walk and not be faint. (Isa. 40:28–31)

Victims find it hard to soar. They sit on tree limbs watching wind-driven leaves fall, twisting in circles and spiraling to the ground. The limb is comfortable. It takes effort and fortitude to *decide* to attempt something that might allow you to soar. It's easier to say, "I'm glad that didn't work out; it wouldn't have been good anyway," than to have tried it and found success or failure.

I've met persons who feel that they are victims of God—that in God's awesome power, God has chosen them to be victims or has decided to punish them. This theology, picked up in the past, doesn't serve them well, especially when difficult events occur and they could benefit from being wrapped in God's blanket of love. Feeling like God's victim calls for asking honest questions about our beliefs *and* wrestling with honest answers. We don't need to have all the answers in life to soar. Honest doubt and wrestling with various answers is an exciting trip in itself, one on which along the way we can fly. Questioning as well as soaring can best be accomplished flying in tandem with an awesome loving God and Creator who is still creating.

I know, life isn't all soaring and rainbows. Everyone knows that there are details, details, details to life, some of which make us feel like ants going in circles. But the colors and textures of soaring make us want to fly on wings of light, wings that can be remembered and tried again and again.

The Parking Lot

Just across the parking lot from the Hurricane Ridge Ranger's Station in the Olympic National Park is a spooky-looking area of hollow tree trunks. Gray ghosts of beautiful trees wiped out by disease, fire, or chemical spill, they are dead, naked of bark, and nothing but bleached wood, yet they are the reminders of things that were. They are things that almost still are, but in a different form.

These gray statues prompted me to think of the ghosts in my life, those remnants of things that once were, things that *almost* still are, the wisps of things just hanging around to taunt. The time I spilled words I never meant to say. The disgust I felt in a certain situation. A failed relationship. Feelings over which I seemed to have no control. A time I was silent but should have spoken up. The times I spoke up when I should have been silent. The ghosts of these events sometimes allow me to wallow in guilt.

Then there are memory tugs of this or that time when someone wounded me personally or professionally. The ghosts of these events could allow me self-righteous anger. I could even harbor a grudge.

Other wisps of things crop up to taunt me concerning illness, mostly things I can no longer do: Swim in the river, play in the symphony, direct a choir, dance with my husband, hold the binoculars for bird-watching. Everyone has ghosts hanging around life, some of them brightly colored memories that bring joy and contentment, but when I noticed the trees, I thought mostly of the gray ghosts in mine.

We all have gray ghosts living in our present—reminders of things that were—that take the color from life and sap our energy. If you are taunted by gray ghosts, join me in turning them to color. For me, the first step was to decide which mental pictures were memories that could enrich life and which were ghosts hanging around to taunt and tease.

Turning the gray ghosts to color takes honesty and some time to dig through them. It's worth the litmus test. My beautiful ninety-five-year-old mother-in-law says that she entertains herself when she wakes up at night by remembering happy, colorful moments from the past. She doesn't seem to remember bad or sad events. What a blessing!

So, hey, color the good memories. Color the river blue-green and cool: Hey! I once swam in the river. Color the symphony black-tie and black dress: I once played in symphony orchestras and can still hear the music in my head. Color the dance floor rose: Maybe by the year 2002 I will dance with my husband again. As for bird-watching: I have developed a great skill of watching the bird-watchers watch the birds. Now there is something with humor, but don't say I told you.

If the obscure ghosts, those reminders of things that were, won't turn to color (it's not an easy process), concentrate on an art-related term for balance. Rembrandt and other seventeenth-century painters used a technique called chiaroscuro, a treatment of light and shade. They used strongly contrasting tones to bring their characters to life. While you're digging through the ghosts, try a little triage. Which do you see in light and which do you see in shade? Which bring light to your life, and which would you like to fade into the background? Put the background fades into an attic drawer or turn them into vapor and make jokes about them. Put the light and colorful pictures on a shelf in your head where you can enjoy them.

Carol Burnett said, "Comedy is tragedy after time passes." Is she right? She has probably learned to vaporize a lot of gray ghosts.

3

Reinventing
PERSONAL THEOLOGY

Each wound to the order of life is accompanied by gashes to the soul that may bring our theology under scrutiny, causing us to deny or reaffirm, redefine, or reinvent. Yet for persons who have little or no knowledge of God, a crisis event may open the way to dialogue and belief in God.

Persons caught in a cycle of turmoil find that they must grow, because new mysteries and consequent questions come at them like shots out of a gun. New questions require answers or redefinition. Such questions drive them to new conversations with God, loved ones, friends, and the Bible. This is active theology, the thinking through or study of God, doctrines, and beliefs. Opening the door to fresh ideas and new interpretations need not be a fearful experience, but a celebration of growth. Beginning the exciting journey can be painful, but it can also become a glorious, continuing adventure.

Make no mistake about the word *reinvent* and its relationship to theology. No one invents God. No one reinvents God. For God is and has been and will be in the future. God does not change. Only our understanding of God changes as we redefine what God means to us in daily life.

Meat Sandwiches

If all you eat for lunch is a carton of yogurt, you may not understand this talk of sandwiches. But if you're a brown bagger who takes leftover meat in sandwiches wrapped in plastic, or if you're an inventive anything-on-bread sort of person, you will understand.

A dainty, teatime sandwich is meant to tide one over until dinner. It does just that, but it isn't suitable for lunch. It just doesn't satisfy or give enough energy to get through the afternoon and sustain the body home on the bus after work.

Meat sandwiches metabolize slowly and sustain energy until the next meal. In meetings people say things such as, "Let's get to the meat of the project," or "Help me find the meat in the budget." They're talking about the good stuff, the substance that gives value and strength to an undertaking or project.

I like this example of substance, the meat of the matter, in understanding what Jesus' stories are about:

> Jesus and his disciples went on to the villages around Caesarea Philippi. On the way he asked them, "Who do people say I am?" They replied, "Some say John the Baptist; others say Elijah; and still others, one of the prophets." "But what about you?" he asked. "Who do you say I am?" Peter answered, "You are the Christ." (Mk. 8:27–29, NIV)

Right on! The meat, the substance! Although Peter still had a lot to learn about what it meant, he had somehow tasted the meat. In adding up the facts and respecting his intuition, he had come to a conclusion that Jesus was the Christ. His answer hadn't happened overnight. Peter and the other disciples had been with Jesus when he drove out evil spirits, healed many, traveled through villages, and stilled the wind and water of a storm. They had protected him in crowds and participated in the miraculous feeding of the crowds. Jesus had taught them using stories with many levels of meaning, which were often misunderstood. Most of that time, the disciples had not fully understood the meat of who he was. Finally, when Jesus asked them, Peter replied, "You are the Christ."

Peter's understanding of what *the Christ* meant was based on traditional beliefs of his day, with expectations of a Jewish anointed king who would come to drive out tyranny. Only living with Jesus, witnessing his death, and eventually coming to know what theologians call *the living Christ* would help him know the meaning of his response, "You are the Christ."

To understand the meaning of Christ, however, makes each of us delve into the history of the word, which is rooted in the Old Testament. Christ is a title, and it is Greek for "the anointed one" or "messiah." The words *Christ* and *messiah* mean the same thing.

For me, the essence of Jesus, the living Christ, comes to life only when I saturate myself with details about Jesus and his relationships with earthly persons as well as the relationship with God he exhibited. I need to study his servanthood, his timeless stories that have grown up with me, their meanings changing as my life experiences and knowledge changes. As a person growing up and as one growing into maturity, I have read and contemplated the records about Jesus in the Bible, and I will continue with great curiosity in the future.

But knowing about Jesus is not the same as getting in touch with the living Christ and handing over control of our lives to him. Patrick, a saint of the Roman Catholic Church, found his way to hand over control of his life. Kidnapped at the age of sixteen (about 405 A.D.) from his birthplace by Irish pirates, he became a devoted Christian while held in slavery. After his escape to France, he became a monk, returned to Ireland, and is said to have baptized more than 120,000 persons. Many legends have sprung up about him, but we know that what he wrote includes the following description of what the living Christ means:

Christ be with me, Christ within me,
Christ behind me, Christ before me,

Christ beside me, Christ to win me,
Christ to comfort and restore me,
Christ beneath me, Christ above me,
Christ in quiet, Christ in danger,
Christ in hearts of all that love me,
Christ in mouth of friend and stranger.[8]

There are many ways to gain the knowledge that Jesus is the living Christ. For Saint Patrick, the glimmer of intuitive spiritual contact came through the hard time of slavery and later to extended biblical study in France and spending his life in the service of Christ. Saint Patrick followed his inclination to reinvent his life. He moved from six years of slavery, having to tend the flocks of a chieftain in Ulster, to spending the rest of his life in servanthood, empowered by Jesus as a role model. He "knew" Jesus.

There are many pathways, and there is much power in knowing Jesus. There are silent, calm, and comfortable "knowings," yet for some persons knowing him is more like an explosion felt from the heart clear to the toenails. Saying "You are the Christ" can be the culmination of studying Jesus' life, death, and resurrection. It can be an intuitive response to an inner stirring of the spirit. It can be a sudden glimmer or sunburst of feeling, or it can mark the beginning of a hunger for finding the meat in the sandwich. "You are the Christ!"

Affirming or reaffirming Jesus as the living Christ can be the beginning of reinventing your life. It may be the most important sandwich you ever eat.

Your Ebenezer

Ebenezer wasn't an old geezer. Originally, the name may have been a place. However, Ebenezer came to be known as the "stone of help" when Samuel set up a stone to celebrate the Israelites' victory over the Philistines (1 Sam. 7:3–13). It was more than a wartime victory celebration. It was more of a "Hey! We wandered away from you, God, and we're sorry" celebration. The stone was a symbol.

What else could they do after such a noisy demonstration? The Israelites, who had seen the error of their ways and had destroyed the idols of their foreign gods, gathered near Mizpah, where Samuel offered water and then a burnt sacrifice. Taking advantage of this, their enemy, the Philistines, encircled them to do battle. The Lord then sent such horrendous, deafening thunder that it threw the Philistines into a panic and they fled with the men of Israel in pursuit.

The victorious Israelites regrouped, and Samuel took a stone and set it in the ground. He named it Ebenezer, for he said, "Thus far the LORD has helped us" (7:12). Gathered around that stone were a bunch of people who had wandered far away from God. Now they had returned to a gracious God willing to forgive and help them.

Sometimes we also need reminders that so far the Lord has helped us. Often when we look to the past with discernment, we are surprised to see God in action in our lives, even when we hadn't noticed. Those who haven't chosen to run with God can affirm that a loving God will walk with them in the future when they invite God to do so.

Do we need an Ebenezer or a stone of help to affirm this walk? Not necessarily, but some people experiencing physical or emotional weakness or theological fragility have discovered that a symbol in their hands or line of vision helps them keep hanging on. I've found that at certain times in life, when things seemed to be going down the tubes and maybe I've wanted to go with them, something to hang on to helps.

Hanging Pegs

There are spiritual hangs, those little pegs we hang our thoughts or prayers on, and there are physical hangs, those things we use as reminders or grasp for dear life just to keep from giving up. Sometimes these hangs are the same.

Many persons use a mental image such as an impressive memory as a reference home base. For example, the Bible does *not* tell us that the Israelites forever carried rocks around with them as a reminder of the Ebenezer experience, but individuals may have carried the mental picture of Samuel standing beside the rock, saying, "Thus far the LORD has helped us." This image pulled into consciousness at stumbling times may have served as a reminder of God's love and forgiveness. The image could cast a new shadow on the future when it gave new perspective to the past.

Another mental and auditory image was important. There is no doubt that the mysterious, deafening thunder remained in the memory of many persons standing around the rock. For some, it may have been a symbol that God is awesome and all-powerful. Other persons may have carried the image of the circle of people around the rock as a symbol of the community of Yahweh believers. Our future interpretation of an event and the image we select to be a peg to hang ideas on are very individual. Our minds seem to have ways of filtering and redefining the mental images that may serve us best.

Mental images are a powerful influence on personal theology. They are so powerful that we may have to move on to a new image as an old one is outgrown. I have moved on to other memory symbols, but a teenage camp experience is as vivid today as it was years ago. I see the night scene, remembering how each individual counselor took a candle and sat near a tree, waiting for a youth to come ask the hard questions of growing up. It was beautiful to watch persons move from the shadows into the dim light to talk about God and ask questions never uttered before. We had been given an open permission slip signed by God *and* the camp director, who said, "Everyone has doubts, fears, and questions about their faith. Tonight and at any time we can ask those questions." Too cowardly to go ask my mountain of burning questions, I just walked around in euphoria, feeling forever free. I wasn't the only one with doubts! It was okay to talk about them! The director's statement forever altered my theology. I discovered that I not only could but also should question as a way of growing in my relationship with God. Even today I can see teenagers going into the circle of light.

More Hanging Pegs

Physical objects may also help us hold on to a sure footing as our theology either needs reinforcement or becomes redefined. A variety of objects can give a solid, grounded-to-the-earth or bonded-with-God type of feeling—objects such as a stick, a miniature cross, a comfort blanket, a book, a fresh leaf, a scrap of paper with a segment of scripture written on it, a hard-won framed diploma, a special pillow, a person's hand, or even a rock.

My friend Pat once gave me a small wooden cross to hold when I was in the hospital too weak to feed myself or lift my head. Why was that cross such a comfort when my heart was already filled with prayer and praise? I have never been able to answer that question, but it felt smooth and reassuring in my closed fist. It must have reminded me of hope, for peace flowed in to replace fear. Not by magic, but by a continuous touch reminder.

Symbols cut through planes of consciousness in individuals, so a symbol will have different meanings for various individuals. Pat tells me that in giving me the cross, the symbol for her was different. She thought of me as holding the cross in my hand while Jesus held my hand in his. Both her understanding of the symbol and mine were based on hope for the future.

We can never fathom the inner workings of the mind and heart that make a symbol significant. Perhaps we need a symbolic Ebenezer stone of help, in any form that is important to us, to help us declare as the Israelites did, "Hey, God! I'm sorry. Walk with me into the uncertain future."

Perhaps now is the time to invite God to journey with us as we redefine or reinvent our theology. Or maybe the best we can do right now is mumble, "Thanks. Stay with me." That's okay, too, if that's where you are in your journey.

Catfish Psychology

I'd rather be fishing from the shade into a cool green river than almost any other activity. I fish for catfish, but I accidentally catch bass and other varieties of fish. Once I caught a seventeen-inch rainbow trout by accident. Using my favorite bait, cheese hot dogs, I recently spent four hours fishing. Although they are usually bottom feeders, the catfish that day for some reason flipped around in the water as I had never seen them do. I knew they were there, because I could see their tails and fins as they broke the water, but they just wouldn't bite. I tried stillness, not moving a muscle. I tried ignoring them while I gazed at the clear, blue sky and the towering, lacy cypress trees. Using an old vibration trick, I sang to them, making up little alto ditties about beautiful green-blue fish. No bites.

Either they weren't hungry, or they were deaf. I've never heard of a deaf catfish; they keenly feel even the vibrations created by walking along the river bank. It's a mystery why sometimes they bite when the wind blows, sometimes not. Often they are hungry when it rains. Then again, often they are not. Often they skitter away when a boat passes over, yet I have caught big fish from under my own canoe. So why weren't they biting then? Catfish psychology isn't always easy to understand.

Maybe they were busy. Busy just doing what they do: being catfish.

Statement or Explanation?

This explanation reminds me of some experiences some friends and I have had with God. Special events in life that call for perseverance or quick action or a monumental decision push a person to God in earnest prayer. We make our requests known. Quietly, we ask for help. Then we yell for help. We sometimes even resort to asking God to wave a magic wand. We try everything—singing, praising, praying longer and louder, seeking understanding of the scriptures, offering better bait (money, chores, service, "I'll change," or "Do it just this once, and I'll never ask again")—with no *apparent* results. We feel out in the cold, alone. What is happening?

My friends and I have concluded that our faith should not depend on instant gratification with a catfish type knee-jerk reaction of "I'll take my bait and go home." We decided that we should accept the present, complete with its many questions, and try to enjoy where we are, even though impatience comes much easier.

Maybe God is just doing what God does: being God. Perhaps, like the catfish, God's not deaf or hungry, but is there. At this moment, God is just there. I find that comforting.

The Pilgrim Path

When the Pilgrims arrived in Plymouth (later Massachusetts) in 1620, their journey wasn't complete. Having endured many hardships on board ship, they thought their pilgrimage was finished, but their search for freedom to worship as they thought proper would continue as they founded towns, built homes, and sought to remain true to their sorely tested beliefs. The Plymouth community was filled with illness, death, bitter weather, extremely hard work, misunderstandings causing internal conflict, and living in crowded conditions. Personally, they reveled in their newly found freedom and the pleasure of founding a community.

We are all pilgrims as we try to remain true to our beliefs, and like the early Pilgrims, we "never fully arrive at Plymouth" without more hardship than we thought. By the time we sort out our beliefs and practices that testify to those beliefs, we get zapped with a new event or idea, and we have to get back to walking the pilgrim path. These personal battles or trials of strength can be viewed as obstacles or opportunities, deserts or oases.

Looking toward the Oasis

The adventure of growth in our spiritual lives can rescue us from the stale sameness that often creeps into spiritual life and pushes us to explore. This adventure can lead to an oasis, a newly found watering hole for persons thirsty for touching God.

Psalm 84 depicts pilgrims coming to Jerusalem, singing. Along the way, arid desert becomes oasis, because God is with them on the pilgrim journey.

> Blessed are those whose strength is in you [God],
> who have set their hearts on pilgrimage.
> As they pass through the Valley of Baca [weeping],
> they make it a place of springs;
> the autumn rains also cover it with pools.
> They go from strength to strength
> till each appears before God in Zion. (Ps. 84:5–7, NIV)

Many other psalms remind us that pilgrims, their hopes and dreams also dashed, have gone before us. Their words become ours as we feel ourselves caught in an arid desert. We may feel that God is far away or has abandoned us. Psalm 43, a prayer for relief from an enemy and for the restoration of God's presence, may sound like a contemporary prayer from a person in the midst of big-time trouble and despair.

> You are the God in whom I take refuge;
> why have you cast me off?
> Why must I walk about mournfully,
> Because of the oppression of the enemy?
> O send out your light and your truth;
> let them lead me;
> let them bring me to your holy hill
> And to your dwelling.
> Then I will go to the altar of God,
> to God my exceeding joy;

And I will praise you with the harp,
O God, my God.
Why are you cast down, O my soul,
And why are you disquieted within me?
Hope in God; for I shall again praise him,
my help and my God. (Ps. 43:2–5)

Three things are needed for a pilgrimage. All three are mentioned in Psalm 43:

I need you.
Send your light and truth to lead me.
I'll remember to play the harp in praise and joy!

People on the Pilgrimage

For thousands of years pilgrims have made the discovery that most pilgrimages never end. And they have discovered the importance of being their best as they go on the pilgrimage, that is, living up to the best that they know. The pathway of pilgrimage is honored by both the present and the future. Pilgrims are both being and becoming. The following prayer is an example of being pilgrim and becoming pilgrim at the same time:

A PATHWAY PRAYER

God
above
and in the world
yet always within me,
show me my path with you.
Enfold me in your care.
Transform me to your likeness.
Let your values be my values.
Let your purpose be my purpose.
Let your name be always in my heart.[9]

Thorn Trees

There has been speculation for hundreds of years about the "thorn in my flesh" referred to by the apostle Paul in his second letter to the Corinthians:

> To keep me from becoming conceited because of these surpassingly great revelations, there was given me a thorn in my flesh, a messenger of Satan, to torment me. Three times I pleaded with the Lord to take it away from me. But he said to me, "My grace is sufficient for you, for my power is made perfect in weakness." Therefore I will boast all the more gladly about my weaknesses, so that Christ's power may rest on me. That is why, for Christ's sake, I delight in weaknesses, in insults, in hardships, in persecutions, in difficulties. For when I am weak, then I am strong. (2 Cor. 12:7–10, NIV)

I'm not big enough or bold enough to say, as Paul did, that I "delight" in my weaknesses or hardships, but for him the thorn was an apt description of "the something" in his life that would keep him humble. He viewed it as an impairment that would help him grow. Theologians, philosophers, and physicians have speculated through the years on what this "something" might have been. Was it a physical or a spiritual malady? Some say it was physical, probably chronic and painful, such as malaria or arthritis, or perhaps epilepsy or myopia. It could have been a short leg or bowed-legs that made walking difficult, a malady that would have been frustrating for someone who traveled as much as Paul did. It might have been bunions that made Paul wince with every step in his travels.

Over the years, some have said it was a spiritual affliction, one that he wrestled with until his death. Was there some deeply hidden doubt about a question of faith, one that burned into his consciousness on frequent occasions, one that stopped him in his tracks? No one knows. But we do know that an empowered, enlightened Paul prayed without question that the "thorn" be removed from his side. Yet whatever the thorn was, it stuck fast.

Gigs and Digs

Most of us have a figurative thorn sticking us in the side. No matter which way we move, it gigs and digs us to make pain in the head, heart, or body. There are more gigs and digs than anyone can count. It may be a relative in jail, an unresponsive child, a parent that bosses us around, or a grief event that won't heal. The gig or dig might be low self-esteem, a dashed dream, an illness that won't go away, chemotherapy worse than the illness, alcoholism or an alcoholic spouse, loss of a career, or even imminent death. It may be a slogan on a tee-shirt proclaiming "Fitness is a witness" when we are not fit, not healthy. We may even design our own tee-shirt that says, "Sickness can be a witness to wholeness, too." After all, Paul was a witness despite his thorn.

There are other minor setbacks that seem major at the time, such as not getting in the university of our choice, losing a best friend, disappointment in a parent, or having a romance terminated. These kinds of pricks hurt, too, and they do not feel like minor setbacks when they are happening.

Personal spiritual thorns also beset us when we don't live up to the best that we know and when we fail to move forward in our faith journey. In the state of complacency and denial we think the thorns are gone until they suddenly reappear, and in desperation we plead with God to "take the thorn away" instead of pleading for company on our faith journey. Sometimes the thorn is taken away, but when the pleading *apparently* doesn't work, we feel the sting of disappointment or guilt. Paul faced a similar situation, but he moved on with his life.

Adaptation and Accommodations

A child with a skinned knee crying to a parent finds comfort, but the child still has to suffer through knee-ooze and a scab that promotes healing. Meanwhile, life goes on. The child goes to school and enjoys the playground. Healing happens. But what about thorny events and experiences that don't seem to heal or that take so long to heal that they spin our lives around?

Trees with spines found in arid regions of the southwestern United States can give us clues about how to adapt to the "thorns in our sides" that make us wince and squirm. When young, the Wright's Acacia is covered with spines as protection against being eaten. After four or five years, when it reaches substantial height above predators, it allocates its energy differently, no longer growing spines. If the tree is injured, it again allocates its energy to spines for protection. Thorny or spiny events in our lives call on us to allocate energy differently, to assess and learn how to wisely and patiently use our energy.

One of these trees growing in the southwestern United States can give us a clue about how to adapt to changing events in our lives. It was growing comfortably in the moist environment of a plain that flooded once or twice a year. Over time, the stream bed moved, and the bush was gradually left in an arid soil. In a struggle for survival, the bush had to adapt. In a few years, the small thorns that once grew straight out from the branches developed into larger thorns, and the thorns turned skyward to catch any mist or dew available to the plant.

There is symbolism in the environmentally adapted thorns that can help us reinvent life when the gigs and digs are getting to us. Like the thorns, we can learn to adapt, reaching toward God for sustenance, wisdom, and comfort that will aid us in any struggle. Like the thorns, we can train ourselves to look up instead of down. It is easy when looking downward to recite the struggle over and over like beads of a necklace until we *become* the struggle. Looking upward not only helps us reach toward God, the optimism found in a loving God keeps life in perspective.

There are also many lessons to be learned from Paul's experience with his thorn affliction. As he said in his writing, unusual, stressful events can help us grow when they cause us to reevaluate where we are in our theology. Whether it's a mental or physical, accidental or deliberate hurt inflicted by someone, we can turn our thoughts to God. We can ask honest, hard questions that open doors to more questions that lead to more thought, and a faith journey is born or furthered.

From Paul we also learn that anyone can be a witness to his or her faith in the midst of severe hardships. Besides his own personal thorn, there were others inflicted on him for thirty years after his conversion. People plotted to kill him and stoned and beat him. He was shipwrecked, put in stocks, imprisoned in Caesarea for two years and in Rome for two more. Paul's not-too-secret weapon, Jesus, made him sufficient to meet the challenges of the many gigs and digs of his life. Careful thought, serious courage, and reallocation of his energy were techniques required for accommodating to even the smallest burdening event.

It Takes Time

One big gulp of an idea doesn't change our theology or the ways we react to a situation. Careful thought and serious courage can help us grow in our understanding of God, an understanding that will be reflected in ways we cope with serious events in our lives. This takes time. Be patient with yourself and the time it takes. The noble southwestern thorns took years and years to adapt in order to survive, and, in the apostle Paul's case, we have the benefit of many years and the biblical writer's interpretations and memories. Paul's was a noble pilgrimage. He reinvented his life over and over by reaching to the source for sustenance, aid, and comfort. He was a scrappy, tough character, and you are, too, but you may not know it yet.

Needed: A Conference Call
(with a Big Speaker, Please!)

Remember the little kid, Samuel, who heard God calling his name in the night? He must have been one scared kid.

Especially when the voice told him stuff that would, as the Bible says, "make his ears tingle." I'd be scared, too. I would also be scared if I said to God, "What do you want me to do?" and he shouted, out loud, some illogical thing. Would I do it even if everyone turned toward the voice, staring at me in anticipation of my doing that illogical thing? I don't know, but I have done some illogical things that intuitively "seemed right." Sometimes I'd say out loud, "You want me to do *what!?*" Emphasize the *what!* Most of the time the *what*'s have turned out to be blessings.

I believe God said something out loud in my head one time. I looked around to see who had called me, but people were going about their business, and no one had even noticed. It could have been a scary experience, but at the time it was a heartwarming and important moment, so important that I wanted a repeat performance. But it never happened that way again.

There are many ways of hearing from God. A friend of mine once had an unusual way. At any time she needed advice, she would put the Bible in her lap, let it fall open, and randomly place her finger at a verse. The verse at the end of her finger became her biblical advice for the situation. Her friends told her that there were better ways to use the Bible, and they urged her to join a Bible study, but she refused. The system worked well for months until one day she read the random verse, "I will send you no more messages." She believed the verse, and she joined a Bible study as a way of hearing from God.

God does, however, send messages in many other ways besides the Bible, and many of the messages are more of an exchange than a one-way directive. In fact, every experience of life may bring a message. I have written some of them down to share. Depending on our personality types, each of us communicates and perceives God's presence and speaking differently, so you can probably add to the list, and you are certainly entitled to question my list.

God speaks in your heart.

- You know God through many inner messages.
- But it would be nice if God said an authenticating password or tweaked your ear or something. Since God doesn't tweak the ear, we all have to learn how and when to listen to the inclinations and messages of the heart.

God speaks through God's Word.

- The Bible's words mean something to you. Lest you think this is one-way speaking, consider that you take the sum of your knowledge and understanding to the reading of God's Word.
- You celebrate the ageless Bible and acknowledge that while the Bible doesn't change, meanings can change with new life experiences.
- But other people may find that the words mean something else.

God speaks through personal sharing.

- You hear experiences of others as they share wisdom or their thoughts or as they tell you what they have been reading. Often, the sharing comes at exactly the right moment to touch and help you.
- But you have to decide for yourself if God is speaking to you or if this is simply a shared story with an unusual message.

God speaks through personal intuition.

- You can know what God is saying without rational process as you contemplate, guess, or know without evidence that it is so. It just seems right. Leadings and inclinations have been well documented, for many of us do this all the time.

- But you have to take time to test intuition. Is it of God? Is it biblical?

God speaks through life experiences.

- You notice that some ordinary happenings and everyday activities give you insight.
- But you have to use great wisdom and discernment and test what has happened and how you interpret it, or things can get out of hand.

God speaks out loud.

- You do not mistake the voice.
- Sometimes you may hear the voice only in your head.
- But it would be nice to have witnesses. In fact, it would be comforting to have the words on a telephone conference call so that your trusted friends could vouch that you've not gone off the deep end.

The main thing is to remain open to hearing God by listening with your whole being. Hearing God with your whole being ends up sounding like the formula for a sermon, planning a Sunday school lesson, or writing curriculum: Focus, Explore, Respond. Focus on God; explore possibilities with God; and once you hear the message, repond. A response is called for, but that is for another page.

Adam's Off Ox

Research for my writing often provides me with little-known facts. When Rika, a character from my teenage novel, comes to Texas, she must walk from Matagorda to New Braunfels wearing heavy brown shoes she hates and driving a team of oxen. I have never driven a team of oxen, so research was important. My most important discovery was that one doesn't drive oxen; while walking to the left of a team, one guides them. Using no reins, a person gives voice commands. This makes life easy if you need your hands for plowing, but can be maddening if you try to keep oxen on a straight trail. If they run away, all you can do is jump up and down and yell at them.

Like many people, oxen are stubborn and balky. They are snail slow, and because they can't sweat, they become overheated and have to be rested until they cool off. Oxen do well feeding on low-grade food, and pound for pound they can outpull horses. A span, or pair, are devoted companions; in fact, the death of one means endless trouble persuading the survivor to work with a new mate.

All oxen recognize one or the other of two names: Buck is the name for the near or left-hand animal in the yoke. Bright is the name for the right-hand animal, and Bright is referred to as the "off" ox. The old expression, "He was as out of step as Adam's off ox," or, "He was roaming as wild as Adam's off ox" might have meant that Adam's right-hand ox was loose and the team was all out of kilter, or it might have meant that Bright was off in the bushes thrashing wildly, and Buck, who had to go along, was confused. Neither was doing any work, and they had probably dragged the plow or wagon off into wild territory.

It is a well-known fact that when oxen hit an obstruction, they don't lunge as horses do; they move steadily, stubbornly forward or, on voice command, go around the obstruction. You might have guessed that there are many object lessons to be employed related to yokes, pulling together, guiding rather than reining, and so forth. My favorite one puts me in a yoke shared with Jesus.

Only two oxen yoked together can pull the load and make the work light and even. If you have been pulling by yourself, you need to hear what Jesus said.

> Come to me, all you that are weary and are carrying heavy burdens, and I will give you rest. Take my yoke upon you, and learn from me; for I am gentle and

humble in heart, and you will find rest for your souls. For my yoke is easy, and my burden is light. (Mt. 11:28–29)

I've heard many interpretations of this scripture, but when I discovered the identity terms and actions for real-life oxen, I began to think that with Jesus in the other loop (for Bright) of the yoke, the leading is focused and easy, and the burden can be lighter and Brighter. And Jesus, in the right-hand yoke, would never be off running away to the bushes. He would lead easily on the road and help pull the burden.

4

Reinventing
WORSHIP

An Italian musical term, *muta,* inscribed on a page of music directs a performer to change the tuning on his instrument. An example of muta is when a player needs to retune the timpani to a new key for the next movement in a symphony.

Not all persons need to reinvent personal and congregational worship. Those who do may need to retune to accommodate for temporary or permanent challenges. There are ways to do this, and you don't have to be a musician to learn to retune.

Sometimes we fall into a comfortable, even routine, pattern of worship in private life and in corporate worship. Any change caused by a stressful event may feel so uncomfortable that we wonder what is happening to us. We may quit reading the Bible, avoid private prayer with all kinds of excuses, or quit going to corporate worship. We may feel sad or confused or lost or any number of feelings that seem strange. When the strange feelings creep up on us, it is time to retune the way we worship.

Retuning requires the skill and courage of looking in a new direction, going into creative thought, and resting in the Lord while doing so. Muta may shake you out of your seat, but it is an opportunity to grow in every direction in worship, perhaps achieving undreamed of heights. Some of this section's ideas may help you with your muta, or retuning.

71

Scramboli

Rube Goldberg, engineer, artist, cartoonist, and the foremost person known for taking a simple operation and reinventing it into something laughable and complicated, said something I like. Not one for learning languages, he said, "Italian is to be eaten, not spoken." Not only do I become engrossed in his silly, beautifully engineered drawings, I relate to Italian food. When someone asks me out to lunch, I have two requirements. One, the restaurant must be accessible for a power chair, and two, "Can it be Italian?" I love ravioli, rotini, cannelloni, fettuccini, spaghetti—all the "i" pastas. It's no wonder, then, that I make up all sorts of fake Italian words, all of them ending in "i."

One of my favorites is *scramboli.* Not Italian and not pasta at all, it's a funny term I use to represent life's scrambled-egg-like events. These are not eggs over easy; they are eggs all broken, shells into little bits, with yolks and whites slimy and mixed up and spread all over the stove. These eggs represent challenging events in our lives. We take our scramboli with us when we sit down to read the Bible at home or pray or just think with God. Scramboli is on our plate when we attend funerals as well as dances. It goes with us to the grocery store and out to lunch with best friends. In short, it becomes part of the pattern of our lives.

The Game of Hide It

To cover our scramboli, we often wear masks that pretend everything is as usual, that stress and grief aren't present, that our faith isn't in question. We look and act as if everything is wonderful, that we are handling scramboli perfectly, but when we sit down to think with God or try to pray, we know that there is no hiding our situation. It's scary. The bedrock of our lives seems to have turned into a geological fault. The result may feel like an earthquake.

More often, and it has happened to me, the scramboli feels like a quiet, hot, dry, flat, endless desert with no geographical or emotional relief. What I have learned about this emotional flatness has helped release me from the stress involved and has kept me moving forward.

If you are in the midst of an earthquake or hot, dry worship conflict, hang on. It's not an unusual occurrence, and it's very healthy to admit that celebrating God is not business as usual.

Scramboli has a way of gobbling energy and time, and often during these events, especially an illness, medication clouds thinking and feeling. In fact, many persons take pills to dull their feelings. And there's no turning away from other life-saving medication that may have this same effect. Even if God *seems* forty trillion miles away, just sit waiting. God is and you are, and the two of you are making connections. Don't fret if you've read the same psalm over and over and can't remember a single word you've read. Keep reading so the rhythm and spirit of the words enter your heart.

During the last stages of Alzheimer's disease, my father was agitated, and I noticed that he could no longer read. When I began reading to him his favorite passages from the Bible, something deep inside him seemed to connect, and he visibly relaxed, eventually falling asleep. Spirituality has triggers. For Dad, it was the comfort and momentary familiarity of words he had read often, an instinctive reaction to something dear to him.

In the midst of fast-paced change events, there may not be much time for sitting in meditation. For example, the best a neighbor, Scranton, could do when his wife left him with four small children was to take segments of time and take a deep breath. He'd say, "Hello, God. You still there?"

Celebration may be a step beyond asking if God is there or simply quietly thinking with God. Too tired to celebrate? Start small, and work your way up as energy returns. Sit quietly using your senses. You may even have the urge to get up out of the chair and actively celebrate.

Celebrate anything that is a blessing. Celebrate something of beauty that you suddenly noticed, an inconspicuous item that entered your awareness. Try focusing on one of these ideas or something similar: your soft chair (snuggle down, feel its texture, and enjoy), sun through a window (put your fingers in its warmth), the drizzly patterns rain is making on a window (place your palm on the cool glass), the feel of cool floor or carpet underfoot (slide your bare feet over the smoothness or scrunch your bare feet against the soft plush), a flower (smell it, feel it, look at the way God created the reproducing parts), or a tree.

Any of these things, a tree, for example, is not just one more growing thing to be celebrated. It is a beautiful, live thing created in God's plan to provide beauty and products for us. Celebration, a point of view, even without our conscious efforts, can turn our thoughts to God.

Picturing individuals may also be a good beginning celebration. Don't be generic. Focus on *one* real person. Perhaps it's your busy, married daughter who has been driving quite a distance to help you clean or cook since your spouse died. Celebrate her caring. Remember her beautiful hair, the way she quietly leaves notes for you. Think about her job. Celebrate her life in detail.

Friends who keep journals tell me that they write about each person they celebrate and have satisfaction in looking back for new patterns and discoveries. Personally, I don't journal in the usual way, but I keep a spiral notebook on which I write lists. With time, I have discovered that my celebration lists often became my prayer list. Celebration can mean anything from a moment of awe to an unexpected smile to an out-loud "Oh, yeah" or a fleeting moment of freedom from pain or stress. Celebration may turn into thanksgiving or growth in appreciation for life, or it may stay pure joy for one particular thing. It's getting outside of yourself a step at a time.

Eggs over Easy

Celebration can't be oversold. Taken in small steps, it may become the walkway of personal worship that leads to reawakening and new confidence. It's a road to somewhere, different places for different people, and even if you don't feel God's presence all the time, persevere patiently. Some day, scramboli will be eggs over easy.

A Kneeling of the Spirit

When you peek at people praying at the altar, what can you see? The bottoms of shoes. Some have new ones, occasionally with the price sticker still there. Others are barely worn, and still others may have holes in the bottom. My father's love for his comfortable church shoes was well known. For years he patched a hole in the bottom with duct tape.

Shoes don't really matter when a person kneels at the altar. But foot disabilities and other mobility impairments might. What if the altar is up steps with no ramp or railing? What if arthritic knees do not prevent kneeling but require calling for a crane with a hoist to get a person back up from the altar? What if debilitating palsy or unintentional tremors means a person will spill the elements? What if someone stumbles over the walker? What if? What if? What if?

Communion and altar time can be a unifying spiritual experience, or it can be scary for persons with "what ifs"—those persons who live with the consequences of impairments. The mechanics of kneeling, walking, stepping, swallowing, and following directions are major problems for a large percentage of any congregation. Also a problem is worry about the "what ifs" that may make a person avoid communion and other liturgical services such as foot washing or carrying offerings to the altar.

Often these problems emphasize differences, and sometimes they bring on pity parties. Seated in my wheelchair out in the aisle at the end of a pew, very much blocking lines of people headed for communion at the altar, I used to have a pity party, until a friend leaned out of line and whispered in my ear, "Have to pay extra for that seat, do you?" People turned and stared when I laughed out loud. I thought of my friend three rows behind me who had to drag his wheeled oxygen tank with him to receive the elements. At least I got to sit. And someone would bring the sacraments to me. That was the last pity party for me in the sanctuary.

Take Responsibility

Since that time I have taken more responsibility for my own corporate worship. If no one holds the hymnal for me, I manage to prop it on my purse in my lap. Because I feel cherished by my congregation, I feel free to ask for help. A minister brings communion to me; if he or she doesn't, I ask for it. When I can't see well, I ask for a large-print hymnal or Bible or worship bulletin. I have also given much thought to what it means to kneel at the altar.

Bow Down before God

Good news for persons with mobility impairments: Communion and altar prayer time don't require actual kneeling. Physical kneeling is an act of humility. It is the "bow down before God" demonstration that God is great, greater than any person or thing. It is an act of personal admission that we are dependent on God. It's an act of soul, an act of the internal spirit more than the body. Isn't it possible, then, that anyone can commit this act of the spirit from a wheelchair or from a seat in the congregation or from lying in bed when one can't get up? Is it not possible that removing the mechanical effort and fear of getting to the altar or standing in line for communion might be replaced by concentration and bowing the spirit before God? Freed of external limitations, a person can attend to confession, repentance, forgiveness, affirmation, and thinking with God, or to any burning issue in need of attention. So sit away. But ask for help if necessary.

A lifetime of kneeling at the altar is a habit that is hard to change, and over and over again a moment of wishful thinking creeps in at the memory of a special moment at the altar. It can be a moment to enjoy before moving to a thought that focuses on the present. Consider clutching an object such as a cross or other symbol as a reminder that kneeling and other acts requiring mobility or physical strength are not the spiritual events involved here. Try thinking about the word *spirit* again and again until it really sinks into your consciousness.

The Loving Touch

Some things come as naturally to a loving congregation as a soft spring rain falling on new grass. A loving congregation may find itself reaching out to touch a person with any kind of special need with a pat on the shoulder or an almost imperceptible touch of the hair. I feel cherished by individuals who touch me on the shoulder or reach to squeeze my hand as they pass. These are usually persons I know. Touching, however, needs to be safe touching within boundaries and only with persons you know will receive the touch willingly. Our Circle of Friends group, one for developmentally delayed teenagers and adults, is a touchy-feely group of huggers. Almost all of us like to hug, but there are a few persons who are disturbed by hugging. We have learned that pointing at each other while establishing eye contact and smiling serves the same purpose as a hug. One young man doesn't want you to hug him; he wants to take your hand and touch it to his cheek. There are physical, emotional, and spiritual touches, so consider what is appropriate to the personality and to the needs of the moment. What if the special need is not visible?

Most people don't realize that emotional turmoil from shattering events can cause worship stress. Coming alone to worship after divorce can be terrifying. Grief from the death of a family member draws persons to a supportive and loving congregation, yet tears are just below the surface. It's hard to sing when there is no song in the heart. What if the mourner begins to sob uncontrollably? What if they faint at the altar? Chemotherapy patients often sit apart from what could be a possibly infectious congregation. Their greatest fear is that with a weakened immune system they might catch something. What if they catch influenza? What if? What if ...?

"What if" fears form roadblocks to corporate worship, so we have to work at getting around them. Although fear can work for us by making us cautious, it can also fester, grow, and block new discoveries. Some fear requires professional help, but fears of "what if" in worship usually are of a different ilk. Recognizing them for what they are can free us to return and reinvent worship. "Turn loose" or "put aside" are mental phrases that can replace "what if."

A Significant Slice of Bread

Go to a major league baseball game alone and sit with fans from your hometown, and you're in like Flynn. There's a bond in common. You can jump to your feet to cheer and yell advice to the umpire. Other fans egg you on.

Don't try yelling advice to the umpire in church, the minister who is preaching, or you may be "ushered out." However, you do cheer for God at a corporate worship service. And, in a way, other fans will egg you on. However, even among this common bond with others at worship, sometimes we can feel alone. It can happen to anyone, but persons with fast-moving or panic events often hyper-focus. We think that the most important thing in the world is the way we *are* at that moment. We might have just gone through a divorce that makes us sit alone, when for years we have been sitting with a spouse. A cancer patient, having lost hair from chemotherapy, may feel that all eyes are on his or her head. A visitor may feel conspicuous. Someone with a broken leg in a new cast may feel clumsy and clatter crutches or have a fear of falling. What it amounts to is feeling different and therefore alone.

Although each of us comes to God alone, we also come to worship God together. A group congregates to acknowledge that God is worthy to be praised. In praising God together, people also acknowledge each other, encourage each other, even cherish each other.

If you ever feel alone during group worship, try the following exercise again and again. Picture yourself as one slice in the middle of a loaf of your favorite sandwich bread. Imagine yourself in a loving congregation as part of the loaf, an important slice. You are significant. Your being here makes a difference. You are surrounded by steadfast love. You are propped up by other slices of bread in the loaf.

Consider this symbolic scripture:

> Is not the cup of thanksgiving for which we give thanks a participation in the blood of Christ? And is not the bread that we break a participation in the body of Christ? Because there is one loaf, we, who are many, are one body, for we all partake of the one loaf. (1 Cor. 10:16–17, NIV)

You may need to feel surrounded and propped in the middle of the loaf by other slices, but in time you may need to hold up persons around you. Thus, you are transformed from the middle slice, propped up by steadfast love, to the useful heel or intermediate slice, holding others upright. You may still feel different, you may *be* different, but in Christ's church you are the same—part of a loaf, an important slice of the body of Christ.

Music as Glue

Music has the power to join hearts. It gives emotional direction and expression to our thoughts, and it can give a new understanding of what it means to be joined as one with other people at church. In other words, music can be an emotional glue. Hard-to-live-with events sometimes make a person feel that the joy is gone from life, and singing sticks in the throat. That's all right; the musical expression of joy will eventually return. Meanwhile, let the music of others sustain you.

There's more to music in the heart than singing with vocal cords. Persons with various impairments contribute to music in whatever ways they can, such as listening, reading the words, swaying in rhythm, or feeling the vibrations. Some play bells or choir chimes or rhythm instruments, wave scarves, or dance. Those who can't read or speak can hum, and some can participate through lining out, a system of echoing one sung line at a time. Vicariously, some may watch the joy on others' faces as they sing. Even if you can't sing, the music of others may make you feel like a significant person within the body of Christ.

If a hard event has troubled your life, and you feel as if the music is gone from your heart and soul, remember the Judeans who were marched into exile. They, like you, felt that they would never sing again. They hung their harps in the willows and mourned their lot in life, their loss of contact with God, and their inability to feel any joy in their hearts that they could turn into song. Yet they again found a new way of life and learned to sing for joy.

Lyrics often present a new understanding of "church fellowship," as they bind people to one another in common praise. A good example is the hymn "God Is Here!"[10]

God is here! As we your people
meet to offer praise and prayer,
may we find in fuller measure
what it is in Christ we share.
Here, as in the world around us,
all our varied skills and arts
wait the coming of the Spirit
into open minds and hearts.

Here are symbols to remind us
of our lifelong need of grace;
Here are table, fount, and pulpit;
here the cross has central place.
Here in honesty of preaching,
here in silence, as in speech,
Here, in newness and renewal,
God the Spirit comes to each.

Here our children find a welcome
in the Shepherd's flock and fold;
here as bread and wine are taken,
Christ sustains us, as of old.
Here the servants of the Servant
seek in worship to explore
what it means in daily living
to believe and to adore.

Lord of all, of church and kingdom,
in an age of change and doubt
keep us faithful to the gospel;
help us work your purpose out.
Here, in this day's dedication,
all we have to give, receive;
we, who cannot live without you,
we adore you! We believe!

Blow Your Own Shofar

Do you have a shofar? Not many people own one or even
know what one is, but it's possible that each of us needs a
figurative shofar blown in front of us. As we read the Old
Testament battle stories, the sound of the ram's horn, or shofar,
mirrors the belief of the warriors that "God is with us!"

The shofar is traditionally a ram's horn, but the horns of the
ibex or antelope were used in the second temple. In present day
usage, the ram's horn is used exclusively in synagogues as a
memorial of the ram that replaced Isaac as a sacrificial animal.

Hardly considered a musical instrument by today's standards,
the shofar can produce only the first two harmonic overtones.
Its function was to make noise, not music. This fact preserved it
after the destruction of the temple in 70 A.D., when all musical
instruments were banished. It was not considered a musical
instrument, so it was allowed to remain in use.

The shofar, or ram's horn, sounded signals for war, peace, new moons, and the beginning of the Sabbath. It also warned of approaching danger or announced the death of a high official. Special musicians blowing shofars walked ahead of warriors into battle; the sound said, "God is with us." It implied, "We are under covenant with God, and he is with us; therefore…"

Constant Change

Faced with constant change and events that shake up our lives, sometimes we feel that we need someone walking ahead of us, blowing a shofar to remind us that God is with us. I don't know anyone who would take that walk for me. Persons who love me would be laughed off the street, and even if they did walk ahead blowing the shofar, I know I would begin to have a better-than-average opinion of myself. "Hey! Here I come. Look at me! Hey! God's with me! Listen to what I'm going to say." This literal use of the shofar could get out of hand.

I guess we'll have to blow the shofars in our heads as a reminder that God *is* with us. Thinking about the shofar can remind us to seek God's direction, which is always revealed to us through persistent prayer but also comes to us in moments of insight as we are caught up in daily challenges.

God Is with Us

Looking back at history helps me keep transition events in perspective, especially when I look for ways and places where God was present.

God was there in the burning bush
    and in the water of the Red Sea
    and on the mountain of tablets
    and in the disappointment of Moses' staying behind.
God was there when armies marched behind the shofar
    and in the temple at the shofar's blowing
    and in the loneliness of captivity
    and in the joy of reinventing life in Babylon.

God was there when Jesus was born in a lowly cave
> and when he talked to the priests
> and when he taught the disciples
> and when he died on the cross.

God was there in the disciples' disappointment at Jesus' death
> and in the joy of his aliveness
> and in the birth of the church
> and in the cold room with Paul while Paul was
> > writing.

God was there last year in our family's marriages and births
> and in daily smiles and anniversaries
> and in the deaths of family members
> and in new discoveries about life and death.

God's footprints are solidly planted on the centuries
> and in our present-day efforts at reinventing life,
> and he has walked in our past year
> and runs with us in the future.

Looking back at our history reminds us that life is always a mixture of goals achieved and not achieved, successes and disappointments. Celebrations and spoken thanks for our successes make us feel good, make our blood race, and make us smile and cheer. We yell, "God was with us!" We may kick our heels together and say, "Hurrah!"

On the down side, however, when a tragic event or disappointment happens, it is more difficult to whisper to ourselves the reminder, "God is with me."

Dag Hammarskjold, former United Nations president, said, "When the morning's freshness has been replaced by the weariness of midday, when the leg muscles quiver under the strain, the climb seems endless, and, suddenly, nothing will go quite as well as you wish. It is then that you must not hesitate."[11]

It is also then that I have learned to blow my inner shofar as a reminder that God is with me. It's not a magical horn blow. It's a mental reminder that I belong to God and that I should always and in all ways seek him as he seeks me, especially when I have found myself in one of life's messes.

Make Your Own Mezuzah

A crisis arises when reality and faith or the practice of it collide. We are looking for solid ground and ways to remind ourselves that we *are* on solid ground. That's when we need a mezuzah. The Hebrews' mezuzah, a touchstone of their faith in God, served as a visible and constant reminder that the house and its inhabitants belonged to God.

In Jesus' day, a mezuzah hanging on a Jewish doorpost proclaimed that the home belonged to God. It was a small case or tube containing a piece of parchment on which was written Deuteronomy 6:4–9:

> Hear, O Israel: The LORD is our God, the LORD alone. You shall love the LORD your God with all your heart, and with all your soul, and with all your might. Keep these words that I am commanding you today in your heart. Recite them to your children and talk about them when you are at home and when you are away, when you lie down and when you rise. Bind them as a sign on your hand, fix them as an emblem on your forehead, and write them on the doorposts of your house and on your gates.

Each person entering the house touched the mezuzah as a reminder that the house and those who lived there belonged to God. Some homes required touching additional mezuzahs as the inhabitants passed from room to room. Touching the mezuzah meant having a personal responsibility to know God and having a measuring stick for values.

Except for some Orthodox Jewish families, twenty-first-century parents no longer keep the mezuzah hanging at the doorpost, but many look for ways to teach of God diligently and to help write the love of God on the hearts of their children. Adults without children also search for ways to keep a mental touchstone of the love of God in their hearts.

Building the Right Environment

Building the right environment, one that will allow a mental touchstone to exist in your home, office, or anyplace, isn't as hard as it sounds. First, you need to know the origin of the word *touchstone.* It is a hard black stone, such as jasper or basalt, formerly used to test the quality of gold or silver by comparing the streak left on the stone by one of these metals with that of a standard alloy. Thus, it was a test of the quality of a thing. It was the "gold standard," or "best test." In building an environment that's right for everyday worship of your God, you need to decide the gold standard of belief. What is the rock bottom? What is the belief that you can truthfully say is yours? Stripped down to its bare essential, what visual and tangible testimonial should your mezuzah proclaim?

A touchstone is not literally a rock, nor is it something you must touch at every doorpost. It should be a simple reminder, visible, just there, a plain presence. Take some time to decide what you need to accomplish through the use of a touchstone. Here's what the mezuzah accomplished:

- It was a declaration of faith in one God.
- It made individuals feel claimed.
- It established family cohesiveness, in which all persons felt claimed by the same God.
- It gave a measuring stick for values.
- It was a mental reminder to hold God in the heart.
- It provided a core belief, a solid-ground place to stand while exploring details of belief.

In addition, there is reference to fixing them [the words of the law] on the hand and as an emblem on the forehead, making direct reference to keeping the religious practice of Jewish law of that day. Contemporary Orthodox Jews still wear phylacteries when they pray, one on the forehead and one on the hand and arm. The phylactery is a small leather box containing strips of parchment on which are written various portions of Jewish law (Ex. 13:1–16; Deut. 6:4–9, 11, 13-21). The phylactery was held in place by leather thongs placed a certain way as prescribed by the law. These served as visible reminders of keeping the law and sent the message to others, "This man belongs to Yahweh."

What touchstones similar in spiritual value can you use to set an environment for the living of the language of worship in daily life?

Reminders

A door plaque showing a fish or cross or the Greek word for love may be the first reminder that comes to your mind. Although the door plaque is truly a proclamation that the house belongs to God and is good advertising for God, the literal act of proclaiming God on the doorpost via a fish or cross is not necessarily the most personal or specific mezuzah you can imagine. This list may get you started:

- a genuine mezuzah
- a stained-glass hanging
- posters
- needlepoint hanging with your favorite scripture
- your current "God's guidelines for life" scribbled in pencil on tablet paper
- an outstanding Bible bookmark
- refrigerator letter magnets (from the poetry kits) formed into your own spiritual growth motto of the year
- a Christmas symbol that is too appropriate to pack away in the attic
- jewelry
- wall hangings
- a special Bible or a spiritual growth word reminder card displayed on an easel

Reminders in Your Home

Whether you have a room in someone's house or live in an apartment, mansion, or fraternity house, it is your present home. And homes take on personalities. James Thurber, an American humorist and writer and an observer of everyday life and behavior, began to see that houses and public buildings had personalities. His illustrations were done in caricatures in which people behave like animals and animals behave like people. Almost totally blind for the last fifteen years of his life, he depended on his emotional responses and sensory impressions to describe the aura of a place. He was convinced that buildings have varied personalities. You probably remember the odors of certain buildings, the sterile chrome and modern furniture or the homey atmosphere of a business or a home with plants and inviting furniture.

Like inside jokes in a family, homes have inside messages they send. Our house has a wall hanging that says, "Laughter is God's hand on the shoulder of a troubled world." A friend's house has an open Bible on the coffee table. It's for real; they actually read the Bible! Some people keep Christian magazines and books in visible spots as reminders that the mind needs value nourishment. They don't spend all their money solely on religious reading, but the spiritual reading does indicate a balance in their thinking. It may be their mezuzah.

Have you thought about what your home says to you? Are there mezuzahs reminding you that you have a walk with Jesus or that God loves you? Are there touchstones that serve as reminders that worship is also everyday life and the way you live it?

Find Your Core Belief

In choosing a symbol or written phrase for a touchstone, you should realize that the process of choosing is more important than the finished product. It may not be a work of art and may mean nothing to others; it is a core to hang on to. Having a core to hang on to allows a person to explore, ask questions, define beliefs and convictions. Holding on tight to that basic belief while looking around allows growth.

In addition to changing your home environment, you may wish to design your own personal mezuzah or touchstone. A symbol or some written words will serve. It's a personal choice. A personal mezuzah might say any of the following or anything you wish:

> God loves me.
> I am wrapped in God's care.
> I am wrapped in God's blanket of love.
> I walk with Jesus.
> (Name), I am your creator and sustainer.
> (Name), I will carry you when you can't walk.
> (Name), I am present.
> (Name), take my hand.
> (Name), you are my child.

Your mind will accept whatever meaning you give an object or group of words. It can be encoded if you do not want family members to understand your struggle at reinventing worship. Try one of the following symbols:

> bell—sound of creative power
> bird, feather, candle flame—spirit
> bridge—link between separate things; transition between one state and another; change
> butterfly—transformation
> circle—completion of cycle; perfection; unity
> cross—intersection of spirit and matter; death of Jesus; salvation for self
> cup—nourishment; abundance
> fire—Holy Spirit; spirit of God alive
> key—access to something locked away; quest for unlocking secrets
> ring—can mean anything, a constant reminder[12]

We all need reminders, and we all need one or more core beliefs. Finding the hard stone of belief on which to stand can help you reinvent honest personal worship. No reinvented life is worth a whisper unless we learn to worship.

5

Reinventing
HOLIDAYS

Clergypersons I know tell me that more suicides and hospitalizations for depression take place around Thanksgiving and Christmas than at any other time of year. Is it because we can no longer see ourselves in these and other holiday celebration pictures we carry in our heads? Has an event changed the entire picture of our lives? Is the holiday picture so blurred that we can't see ahead?

There are reasons to go deeper into real meanings of designated holidays while changing the expectations we carry in our heads. And it is possible to reframe former family gathering pictures, giving them new meanings.

Success at reinventing and learning to enjoy personal holidays and family gatherings requires finding a way to fill the vacuum of what we did before a drastic event of change entered our lives. There's a stepping stone down there someplace where we can stand on a core belief while exploring how we will celebrate.

For Sale: Sacred Relics

This year I started Lent a few days late. Lent is a time when individuals and congregations prepare for Easter, originally a teaching and searching time. For the earliest Christians it was a time of preparation for baptism at Easter. As centuries of church societies progressed, Lent took on new definitions, rules, and boundaries. Even contemporary churches continually find fresh ways to peer into the meaning of Christ's death and resurrection. They invent new rituals in an effort to make Easter more meaningful for the average person. A period of thoughtfulness and darkness is followed by lilies and banners and singing and joyous proclamations. Usually I participate in the services.

But this year is different for me. I am unable to join the endless line of Christians obtaining ashes. And I am unable to join the singers and celebrators recalling the stories of the meaning of Easter. So I have decided to take a personal look at Easter in a new way. *What would it mean if the event happened today?*

The Essence of Easter

No doubt about it, a present-day death and resurrection would make the six o'clock news, and by morning there would be religiously correct points of view every few hours presented by a wide range of organized believers, nonbelievers, or disbelievers.

As in the early post-Jesus days, Christians would be claiming that they have discovered a different way of life that is better than that offered by the non-Christian world. Then the fun would begin, with disagreements all around about what the good news or better way of life means. Electronic media would flash the news; cybernet users would interpret it; commentators would probe meanings and affirm or discredit the event.

Disciples would be denied time to grieve and sort out the meaning of the death of Jesus. They would make guest appearances on *The Today Show* and every other talk show. No one can know what effect the appearances would have. After Jesus appeared to the disciples, reporters who followed along for a story would have their lives changed depending on whether or not they believed what they saw and felt.

The stone rolled away from the tomb would be chipped into bits much like the Berlin Wall, perhaps to be sold over the Internet. Sacred relics such as splinters from the cross might even be hawked and bought by a populace with mixed intentions, some buying souvenirs from a bad joke, some serious buyers wanting a sacred reminder, and some buying because everyone else wants them.

I am profoundly glad to live now, times away from the event of Jesus' death and resurrection, with the benefit of the great thinkers of the ages who have put these events into perspective. I am thankful for my childhood memories and training about Easter. Sunrise services and community Easter celebrations with orchestra and chorus give a sacred perspective to the Lenten season. I also celebrate the centuries of saints and great philosophers who have helped me interpret my life under the Easter umbrella.

Thank you, God, for your painstakingly collected and laboriously written down words in the Bible that serve me as guides to understanding the meaning of the new creation and Christ-like qualities. Thank you, God, for the persons of great spiritual insight who over the years have held the Easter event up to the Sonlight for examination and meaning. Thank you, too, for preserving their ideas and giving me the opportunity to hear or read their thinking. Thank you, too, for redefining yourself through the gift of Jesus and his resurrection. Yeah, God, and Amen.

Everyone enjoys and feels comfortable celebrating Easter with rituals and events they have used for years. Those are wonderful, but they are communal celebrations. This year, add a new and different form of celebration by going into the spiritual and creative realm, asking the question, What does the Christ event of Easter *mean* for me today?

Celebrate the preservation of the story by reading it from different authors: Mark: 14:32—16:20; Luke 22:39—24:12; Matthew 26:47—28:15. Read all four gospels in order to understand the essence of the life of Jesus as well as his death and the greatest of all reinventions, the resurrection.

Pajamas for Christmas

You know you're growing up when suddenly both grandparents stop sending toys for Christmas. It's such a shock when, on Christmas morning with everyone watching, you tear eagerly into the paper on the big box, open it, and gasp. Pajamas! And a matching robe! You try to hide your disappointment. You say thank you. But you're thinking, "How ordinary."

Clothes are the marking line for a little less kid magic in Christmas, the line when grandparents think that you're too grown up for more toys. A kid knows, though, that she may be too old to *ask* for more toys, maybe another doll, but that is exactly what she wants. Shyly trying to admit that she is growing up, a kid doen't ask for the doll. Suddenly, toys are out. Santa Claus is out, and Jesus may be in, so it's a time to be serious about Christmas.

At such an un-asking-for-toys age, Christmas seems to be in transition, and a person has to figure out what the actual birth of Jesus really meant. It was a simple but not ordinary event.

During the early teen years persons learn that Jesus was the gift of God himself in a new translation—a gift that has never been surpassed. The story seems too full of miracles. It's hard to wrap the mind around.

The Miracles

The whole idea of Jesus is one big miracle. It's a miracle that God pulled it off. First, it was the Holy Spirit's idea, not Joseph's. Now that's a big-time miracle!

Second, it's a miracle that Mary wasn't scared out of her wits into a miscarriage. And can't you just hear the conversations in her head? "No one will believe this. My family and friends will say I've been fooling around." Or she might have talked to herself: "What will Joseph say? He can divorce me. Who will feed this child and help me take care of it? What will this child look like with no actual father? Will it be human with eyes, nose, and mouth, or a huge supernatural blob? If no one believes me, this child will be a bastard—shunned."

Third, it's a miracle that Joseph believed Mary and didn't divorce their engagement. He, too, probably talked to himself. "Mary was so proud and beautiful when we became engaged. She was young, inexperienced, full of life. Now, during the betrothal period, she hits me with this. She will always look different to me." The worst thoughts whirling in his head might have been, "My family will think I have dishonored Mary before marriage. So will my friends. My honor is at stake here."

How amazing that Joseph believed the dream message recorded in Matthew 1:20–21:

> An angel of the Lord appeared to him in a dream and said, "Joseph, son of David, do not be afraid to take Mary as your wife, for the child conceived in her is from the Holy Spirit. She will bear a son, and you are to name him Jesus, for he will save his people from their sins."

What a wonder that he didn't wake up and say, "I shouldn't have eaten that greasy meat just before I went to bed." Can you imagine how sobering his next thought might have been? "When an angel calls me by name, even in a dream, I guess I had better pay attention." God must have given him the inclination to pay attention and believe.

I've always been fascinated by the miracle of the wise men. There may have been as many as a dozen or as few as two. Often called sages or magi, these were men of science, probably teachers of kings who understood dreams as revelation and believed that birth stars held clues about a person's destiny. Of the gospel writers, only Matthew includes the wise men story. It's a great one.

Matthew made a universal appeal. To me, it really seems to be a miracle that the wise men, after meeting with Herod, defied him and went home another way. It was sort of a birthday present for Jesus. No ordinary pajama gift from them. Instead, having achieved their purpose, they gave a magic disappearing act.

One more miracle inspires me. Joseph was told in a dream to take the family and flee to Egypt. And he did. Perhaps he had become accustomed to angels and bright stars and dazzling ideas by this time. But he must have wondered, "Will everyone think I'm so scared I have to run? My parents may think we are dead! And how will I provide for my family in Egypt?"

Because God created us with free will, the success of God's awesome plan for the birth of Jesus depended on placing in the hearts of Mary, Joseph, and the wise men the *inclination* to believe these many miracles step-by-step.

One of my Christmas questions is, "What miracles does God have in mind that depend on my inclination to act?" I must get ready for miracles today, expect them tomorrow, and have the inclination to see them.

I may not see them at first, especially if I receive ordinary pajamas instead of toys. I have to get past Santa, toys, and selfish wishes and grow up. Well, everyone has to keep growing up.

Want to access the grown-up miracles of Jesus' birth yourself? Read Matthew 1:18—2:15.

Let's Talk Turkey about Family Gatherings

Hope springs eternal with me. Every Christmas day, surrounded by mounds of crushed red and green wrapping paper and snarls of gold ribbon, I promise myself that next year I will be more prepared, more thorough ahead of time, more relaxed and less tired. Yes, I know it's pie-in-the-sky and pigs do fly; just the same, I make the resolution.

People make resolutions around family gatherings. Some of them can be kept, and others are laughable. Not that family gatherings are gloom and doom, but there are as many reasons for depression and unhappiness around holidays and other family gathering times as there are people. Family gatherings can be happy, yet some just *seem* joyful. Relatives joke with each other, and a lot of the entertainment centers around food and its preparation. It's a safe starting point. Or is it?

At family gatherings, things are not always as they seem. Civility is important, but we may need to tune our sensitivity radar. Teasing about Cousin Jake's lazy, "store bought" potato salad, your brother-in-law Jackson's new car, and Aunt Minnie's hot-as-fire stuffed mushrooms keeps people entertained. Smoldering underneath may be layers of hidden fears and wounded self-esteem.

> Cousin Jake brings "store-bought" potato salad, a no-no in his family, because arthritis in his feet hurts so badly he can no longer stand to cook. He mostly eats fast-food or the occasional TV dinner. His foot condition has worsened since his wife died, but he won't mention it today because his children might think that he needs to make a change in his living quarters. Supporting himself by moving from chair to table to a wall, he gives the appearance of robust health. His feet remain his secret.
>
> Jackson also has a secret. Every family reunion for five years has left him smarting from teasing about his jalopy, the one with the dented fenders and the hole in the floor. No one knows that the good-natured ribbing is, for Jackson, a constant reminder of his financial failure. A little part of his self-esteem is torn away every year as he jokes away about his love for the old car, a blatant lie because he hates the car. Today is different. Now he has money, because so far he has been lucky. But now he is addicted to gambling. He hopes that the

addiction will remain his secret, but what if someone recognizes him from a casino?

When the jokes about calling the fire department for the mouths burning from the hot mushrooms die down, Aunt Minnie confides to Jake that she is losing her eyesight and can't read the spice labels. Chili powder looks just like paprika, she says. Jake puts his arm around Minnie's shoulder and nods his understanding. Her independence is up for grabs, too. She has a secret, and he shares his.

These are usual happenings that have already changed and will change many family dynamics. There is no right or wrong way to deal with these subtle changes. Families will deal with them in ways that are comfortable. Some will pretend that there are no problems, choosing only to share joys, thus seeming to preserve the dignity of persons with problems. For example, Jake might offer Aunt Minnie transportation without mentioning her eyesight, and she may even exchange the ride for a casserole or pot roast. Other families will share the good and the bad, choosing to encourage and embrace each other, making accommodations here and there. This family type may also wonder why certain persons are missing from the family gathering. But all families are different, as all persons are different.

Drastic Changes

Missing from the circle may be a person whose life has undergone drastic changes that have upset the equilibrium of family dynamics. For that person, socializing may be painful. The ritual of celebration may now be so lopsided or out of kilter that participation would be distressing.

At the top of the list of drastic Change is *divorce* and/or *battles for custody of children*. Everyone suffers. Everyone grieves. All persons involved have to take time to sort out actions, reactions, and abandoned or forbidden relationships. Grandparents often deplore the actions of their children, but they must represent loyalty to their own child and may be cut off from a child's beloved spouse and children. Holidays often become battlegrounds for child custody as well as competition for overabundance in giving. The overwhelming complexity of getting together creates confusion. Even worse, the reality of not joining the family creates loneliness or depression or both.

Also on the list of drastic changes is *unemployment*. A full-scale family gathering always includes questions such as, "What are you doing now?" or "Where are you living?" Painful answers include, "I have moved back in with my parents," or "I'm between jobs," which is an optimistic answer unless you've used it previously and have to admit, "I'm still looking for a position." Amazing as it may seem, relatives always have suggestions that are low-paying or that do not fully use your skills, such as an advanced degree. The pain of rejection or embarrassment keeps many unemployed persons alone during the holidays.

Grief, fresh or unresolved, makes explaining how you are dealing with it unspeakable. To speak is to dredge up. To dredge up is more than uncomfortable. A friend whose famous husband died just before Thanksgiving confided in me the number of holiday dinner invitations she had received. To each she replied that she had other plans. "What are you going to do?" I asked. "Thanksgiving is for their families. I'll be very comfortable alone." "What will you do?" I asked. She thought only a moment. "Something I have always wanted to do on Thanksgiving. Not cook. I'll take my ham sandwich, chips, and coke and hide under the dining room table in case anyone rings the doorbell." She later told me that the day was full of happy memories played over and over, and she definitely loved not standing at a sink peeling yams. She is, of course, not stuck under the dining room table for years to come, but she chose her own way to deal with the grief of a holiday alone.

It isn't easy to admit that *physical and mental impairments* tilt the scales of balance at family gatherings. Among the greatest stressors is the loss of communication skills, especially the ability to hear. Misunderstandings come easy, and people seem to think that yelling will make it better. Persons with hearing aids find that crowds are noisy and create static, painful sounds, and Fourth of July fireworks may sound like a blastoff at Cape Kennedy. Is it any wonder that persons who are deaf or hearing-impaired often choose to avoid family gatherings?

Mobility impairment becomes an obstacle to attending some family functions. My wonderful family have built ramps into their homes, enabling me to ride my wheelchair to family get-togethers, but many persons with other impairments find that they have mixed feelings about a crowd, even a crowd of loved ones.

In spite of these and other obstacles to feeling comfortable and available for family events, there are reasons to stay within the family cocoon or circle whenever possible, even at great personal sacrifice. That may mean swallowing pride or being honest when it would be easier to lie.

More than Big-Eating!

Family dinners, reunions, and holiday celebrations are more than back-slapping and big-eating. They represent regularity, cohesiveness, and a pattern of culture already in place to benefit individuals and groups. They represent loyalty and belonging. Within these groups children and adults learn from one another; suffer deaths of loved ones; witness their religious beliefs; and promote and encourage rites of passage such as baptism, school graduations, marriages, and births of children. The family members (and extended family, those at a distance who come together perhaps once a year) undergo change, learn to react to change, and experience joys and sorrows while supporting one another.

Families develop patterns in the ways they act and react, patterns copied by families within the family, and for the most part, this learning handed from generation to generation is beneficial and comfortable. These are the reasons to participate within the family circle whenever possible. I mention them before addressing the downside of family gatherings for a special reason.

What about Change Events?

When events of drastic Change happen and new patterns of operation *must* be reinvented, it is important to fill the vacuum of what one has left. The family circle, large or small, has had characteristics often unnoticed. Now is the time to notice the many unstated benefits and keep the positive ones as goals for the future. New liturgies and symbols must be replaced or carried on with a different set of relationships. It's work that should be intentional. Pay attention to the kinds of patterns you wish to establish. In order for them to be healthy, consider the following: Establish new memories, form new loyalties and preserve as many old ones as possible, find new ways to celebrate personal or family joys, establish support for new ways to encourage people in life crises, find fresh ways to share values and religious beliefs or make an effort at continuity in long-standing values and beliefs. At first the intentional tasks may feel strange, but as the vacuum fills, the patterns will be established joyfully.

Let's be honest. For some families the pattern of operation may have been accompanied by disagreements and mis-understandings that sometimes drove persons apart. Some families hold to perfection, allow no differences, and are judgmental. Reinventing holidays provides opportunity to improve. And when all is said and done, after time, returning to the original happy circle may be possible. Then again, it may not. Instead of turkey, Thanksgiving might mean hot dogs over a mountain campfire. That's okay too.

6

Reinventing
HEALTH AND WHOLENESS

It's true! We learn from a past that holds both joy and sadness. Hope helps us look to the future while enjoying wisdom from the past. Hope drives us to seek wholeness and allows us to strive for health.

There's hope! We're Not Humpty Dumpty!

Unlike Humpty Dumpty, the egg who sat too near the edge and fell, smashing himself into fragments that couldn't be put back together, we can find a glue to fix ourselves. Broken bones, broken trust, dashed dreams, and hurts of many sorts need the glue of healing and wholeness. The Holy Spirit may be the glue that works within us in mysterious and unexplainable ways. Or the glue may be walking with Jesus or…or…There is a glue for you.

According to the dictionary, *whole* or *wholeness* refers to "a thing complete in itself." A whole person, then, would be integrated, balanced, and healthy in spiritual grounding, thus complete. It is possible to be unhealthy, imperfect, homeless, poor, rich, or just different while being whole at the same time, but becoming whole isn't automatic. It's a choice, and we have to be intentional.

Some of this section's ideas may help you learn the power of wholeness and how it relates to health.

Boy! Do I Have Connections!

Everyone who is reinventing life can joyfully celebrate the blessed connections that ease the reinvention. Giving thanks doesn't hurt, either.

I have never seen the queen of England, but my husband, Bob, has. She established eye contact and waved at him as she passed by in a London parade. I have never met the president or even the governor. I don't even know many important people, and could never be a name-dropper if I wanted to; I'm so un-connected with famous people that I wouldn't know what names to drop.

But I rejoice in the connections I have been allowed. There are reminders all around me of family, friends, and recreational and professional connections that have enriched my life. There are the Plowmans, junior-high church counselors, who made spiritual growth fun and maybe didn't even know the long-term effects of their efforts. There was Ed Royse, who taught me the power of serving others. There was Letha, a Bible scholar who could translate her knowledge into daily doings and speak of Jesus as if he came to breakfast every morning. There was Sid, who asked me, "Who tells you who you are?" and didn't give me the answer, leaving me to figure it out for myself. My connections go on and on. Yours probably do too.

Jewels from the Past

Jewels from the past have helped me grow into reinvention. One of my powerful connections comes from books. As I connect with both contemporary authors and those of ages past, I feel a kinship with them and thank them for sharing their thoughts.

Picture this scene from a favorite biblical writer connection of mine: The apostle Paul has been under house arrest in Rome so long that he lives in a rental house where people may come to him, but he may not go to them. Money for his expenses has been sent from a group of Christians at Philippi.

While Paul is one of *my* "connections," he is busy writing his thanks for *his* "connections" to Christians who have supported him not only with money but also with confidence in his cause and teachings. He says to them:

I thank God for you Christians at Philippi whenever I think of you. My constant prayers for you are a real joy, for they bring back to my mind how we have worked together for the Gospel from the earliest days until now. I feel sure that the one who has begun his good work in you will go on developing it until the day of Jesus Christ.

It is only natural that I should feel like this about you all—you are very dear to me. For during the time I was in prison as well as when I was out defending and demonstrating the power of the Gospel, we shared together the grace of God. God knows how much I long, with the deepest Christian love and affection, for your companionship. My prayer for you is that you may have still more love—a love that is full of knowledge and wise insight. I want you to be able always to recognize the highest and the best and to live sincere and blameless lives until the day of Jesus Christ. (Phil. 1:3–10, Phillips)

Can't you imagine the surprise on Paul's face if anyone had told him that two thousand years later people would be reading the letter he wrote to the Philippians while he was in prison? The legacy of his thoughts and the records of his actions are treasures.

I have never been in a state-run physical prison, but, like many other people, I have been prisoner of my own thoughts many times. Connections to historical persons can often help one see the bars on windows of the mind. The same connections can also help remove those bars.

Boy! Do I have a connection to Eusebius. Have you ever heard of him? He was born in Palestine about 263, was on the run during the Great Persecution, and was later imprisoned for his faith. He became bishop of Caesarea and was a historian and writer. One of his writings, *Church History,* is priceless for its grand-scale descriptions, extracts, and quotations from otherwise lost works. Although Eusebius was not the first church historian, only fragments of other authors' works exist. So Eusebius gave me connections to the disciples and persons in the early Christian church.

Flavius Josephus, an important Jewish historian, was born in Jerusalem only four years after Jesus was crucified. As an eyewitness of the times, he reported a lot of what happened in the first century, and he supplied details not found in other writings. Josephus had intimate connections to historical facts and provides the modern reader with details that enhance Bible study. His work is difficult for the modern casual reader to follow, but it has been translated without changing its main ideas.

As Christianity moved through the ebb and flow of critical thinking, many philosophers and religious thinkers argued for supremacy of reason, authority of the Holy Spirit, and the authority of the self-interpreted Bible. They investigated and survived heretical sects; helped define the sacraments; watched totalitarianism, nationalism, and other ideologies, speaking and writing to the benefit of Christians everywhere. My connections to persons involved in these writings exists even when I haven't read everything written on these subjects. I benefit from their knowledge accumulated in libraries they have never seen, a gift they didn't know they were giving me, a gift from the past with possibilities for my future.

Other jewels from the near past may take a little personal digging. When great changes smash into our lives, sometimes the past gets blurred or tilted out of focus. Regain that focus by picking through childhood, teenage, and earlier adult jewels of joy. A scrapbook or letters, even a medal or old grade card will trigger such memories. Examining these *positive* (ignore the negative for the moment) experiences can provide a clear emotional frame of reference that can bring the present into focus. Thinking clearly promotes wholeness.

Jewels of the Present

Medical connections have been a valuable tool for me. Through connections with the persons who developed magnetic resonance imaging (MRI) and computed tomography (CT) scans to Doppler readings of the body and pills for almost everything, most of us owe great debts of gratitude for hard-won medical advances. Everyone who is reinventing life can be thankful for the blessed connections that ease or further these inventions.

The list of connections is as long as the list of fast-moving events, perhaps even longer. Connections stretch from the person who developed new and better artificial limbs to psychologists, writers, teachers, friends with soft shoulders, and the bus driver who smiles at us in the midst of what some persons might perceive as a gray world. The connections extend through the Holy Spirit, who warmed our connections in the past and wraps us in colored blankets of love in the present. Giving thanks for all these connections causes one to celebrate life. Celebrating life is part of being whole.

The Cloverine Salve in Gilead

When I was growing up, everyone said that Cloverine Salve would fix about anything from poison ivy and boils to acne and a scraped knee. Cloverine came in a pretty white tin box with a green four-leaf clover on the lid and green writing around the edge. Not available at any local store, it had to be ordered from a catalog, and fine print on the catalog cover suggested that anyone of any age could earn bonus points by selling the medicinal products in the catalog.

This was good news for me. For two years I had yearned for a violin. I thought about it day and night, prayed for it, longed for it, and suddenly discovered that for only 150 bonus points I could earn a violin, bow, and carrying case. That meant selling 150 white tin boxes of Cloverine. In a matter of weeks, I was in business. Grandmothers, aunts, uncles, cousins, neighbors, schoolteachers, and friends at church coughed up money for the cure-all. I walked on cloud nine, picturing myself sitting in the beginner orchestra playing my beautiful violin.

All was not well in orchestraland however, when word got out that the sweet-smelling Cloverine seemed to be merely petroleum jelly and scent. It could soften calluses, my clients said, but it had no healing powers at all. After thirty-nine sales, I stalled out, eventually paying postage to return 111 tins.

The violin materialized only when Mother took in washings to earn what she knew was my heart's desire. It took a lot of buckets of hot water carried to the old Maytag. I call this experience my Cloverine discovery: Be careful of a quick fix. It takes time and hard work to get what you want, and it helps to have a love figure shouldering the burden.

Where's the Balm?

Every one of us is looking for a salve of healing. We want a bit of magic that can skip the stitches and bandages and go to welded flesh without a scar. If we're sick, we want a God Balm to make us instantly well. If we have a wounded psyche, we wish for a quick fix balm. If we wrecked the car, we want the insurance to pay it off within this very week. If we are scheduled for a speech at a Rotary Club, we may pray for a theme for the speech and plead with God to send the ideas by Thursday night because the speech will be Friday.

Although I believe in instant balm (it's more like a one-day, highly effective antibiotic), it may be the exception. In my experience, there's great healing balm in the process or longer-term cure, that of pushing onward toward a genuine walk with Jesus.

Because I love to sing "There Is a Balm in Gilead," I have thought about my Cloverine discovery and have tried to understand the operations of time and hard work and the Holy Spirit's revival in verse one.

The refrain for "There is a Balm in Gilead" is as follows:

There is a balm in Gilead to make the wounded whole,
there is a balm in Gilead to heal the sin-sick soul.[13]

After I sing the song, the words "There *is* a balm" echo in my mind the rest of the day. Sometimes it goes on a loop around and around until I wish it would go away, but mostly I find those beginning words reassuring. The wonderment of the fact that there really is a balm makes me smile.

This African American spiritual warms my heart. I love it! Who hasn't been wounded? Who hasn't been drowning in guilt and had a sin-sick soul? Who doesn't need Jesus as a friend? I've been in all of these places. But I kept wondering about the balm. What was it literally and figuratively in biblical terms? And what is the modern-day balm of Gilead?

The Ancient Biblical Balm

Curiosity led me to discover some facts about the biblical balm. It is resin from a shrub-tree found in the geographical area of Gilead, east of the Jordan River. The balm or salve was used in ointment for wounds, or as incense, or as an embalming substance. In biblical times the ointment was so well known that it became a figurative reference to what we would call an over-the-counter remedy, sort of an effective Cloverine Salve of its day. Today we think of a balm as something that soothes, heals, or mitigates pain of any kind.

The prophet Jeremiah used a figurative reference to the balm. He was doleful, pessimistic, and overbearing and won no peacemaker awards in his time. As God's spokesman he stirred things up so much he was beaten and thrown in jail. Later, when his predictions had come true and most people had been carried into Babylonian captivity, his talk-talk-talk mouth was still getting him into trouble, and those left behind threw him down a cistern. Luckily, the bottom had no water but lots of mud, and he mired down to his armpits. To his surprise, no one was eager to rescue him.

Unpopular as he was, however, he was God's spokesperson; he did get out of the cistern, and he carried out his duties with persistence. Deported to Egypt, he continued his prophetic utterances regarding Egypt (Jer. 46:11).

What he said had the ring of truth, and having suffered and probably used the Gilead balm without prescription, he referred to it regarding Babylon. Suggesting that perhaps medicine, the balm of God, might heal Babylon, Jeremiah concludes this section of scripture with the declaration that the Lord has vindicated Israel and that they should declare in Jerusalem all that the Lord their God has done (Jer. 51:10).

Jeremiah's stories and his reference to balm force us to look at what might be hard work connected with the balm of Gilead. What he said was, "When you examine your life, face the truth, and ask forgiveness, you can get right with God. It will feel like the balm from Gilead. It will heal old wounds and soothe the national soul" (author's paraphrase).

The balm, then, might be that God steadies you by putting his hand on your shoulder. He gives you the courage to reevaluate your life and helps you make order out of confusion.

Balm Formula

Your formula for finding the balm may be different because life experiences differ, but this one has helped me and is worth trial and commitment:

1. Examine your life with the help of the Holy Spirit. You will be encouraged.

   Sometimes I feel discouraged and think my work's in vain, but then the Holy Spirit revives my soul again.

2. Face the truth. This is often the hardest part of the formula. (It certainly was for Babylon and the Israelites.) Although we usually think of peering at truth as revealing our sins or

bad habits, we must also be willing to accept good and encouraging truths, even when we are down on ourselves. Acknowledging the positive truths can be difficult. True knowledge of self is never one-sided.

Don't ever feel discouraged, for Jesus is your friend;
and if you lack for knowledge he'll ne'er refuse to lend.

3. Ask forgiveness when necessary.
4. Get right with God, the soothing balm! Feel God's hand on your shoulder.
5. Declare what God has done. It's a testimonial for the balm, and Jeremiah says that the Israelites are to declare all that the Lord has done.

If you can't preach like Peter, if you can't pray like Paul,
just tell the love of Jesus, and say, "He died for all."[14]

What is the balm? What do you think today? Try the list again next week and next month. Make a checklist from the following. The balm is:

- Jesus walking beside me.
- God's hand on my shoulder in such a way that I feel extremely loved.
- God's presence within me, giving me courage to go on.
- God's action alive in the world and in those around me.
- Being able to free myself from inner terrors by telling them to God.
- Finding balance and integrity in life.
- Saying, "God is great and God is good."
- Saying, "God, I depend on you."

There *is* a balm in Gilead that has helped people reinvent their lives and renew their faith. It's available to anyone who wants the product and who will issue an invitation: "I'm ready for the balm."

Giggles and Belly Laughs

I always felt happy around Lilly, one of Grandma Phoebe's friends who giggled all the time. She prefaced every sentence with a "tee-hee" and added the light touch of good nature to all Grandma's quilting parties. Much to the discomfort of our family, my sister and I caught her giggles. We became giddy with apparent good nature. We drove everyone crazy with our constant giggles and tee-hees until finally we were ordered to be serious and quit that silly giggle. We did quit, sort of. However, after fifty years, the giggles still crop up. I found that the giggles weren't just a bad habit. Lilly and Grandma Phoebe taught me something about attitude toward life, the same thing my children meant when they said, "Come on, Mom, lighten up."

Eric Berne, father of transactional analysis and author of *Games People Play,* said it differently. To be truly alive, persons have to learn to kick up their heels. He says, "Wholeness is the ability of a person to say, 'Yes!' 'No!' and 'Whoopee!'" He defines sick people as those who say, "Yes, but...," "No, but...," and who cannot say whoopee.[15]

Not everyone can say "Whoopee" all the time, but let's face it. Reinventing life day by day or as necessary can get heavy. If we can spin some humor into it and lighten up, the trip can be more enjoyable, and there are many benefits.

Keeping Life in Perspective

Over the years I have realized the significance of laughter and having a humorous viewpoint in keeping life in perspective. Life presents us with enough killer events to keep us glum. However, glum keeps the eyes downcast, keeps the corners of the mouth down, shifts our energy gears into slow motion, and discolors the way we see things. Getting past that and placing a humorous spin on an event can help us see the situation in a new light.

A humorous spin releases tension and helps us maintain mental balance. The spin may occur during a tense event or after a reasonable amount of time has passed. Carol Burnett said it well: "Comedy is tragedy plus time."

In one example of instant amusement, police in the northwestern United States helped pull a miraculously uninjured man out of his cratered car, which had rolled two times. His first question was, "Are my tires flat?"

A case of late-blooming humor came when our Texas Hill Country vacation home was completely covered by floodwater. Inside the house were dead fish, mud, sewage, fallen-in drywall and insulation, and all our ruined furniture. On the roof were telephone poles, fences from someone's yard, driftwood, and piles of strange debris. No electricity, water, phone, sewer, ramps, or even a place to park my wheelchair. Where's the humor? Later, when the sun finally came out, we found a few jokes. Nestled on some trash at the roof's peak rested one bright blue, sparkling clean and reflective Christmas ornament. What a funny trick of Mother Nature!

Inside the house, a soggy, striped picnic basket had floated onto the blades of a ceiling fan and rested there, dripping colored water on our heads as we shoveled mud. We laughed belly laughs (the kind that shake your stomach and your soul) and took pictures of it and of the heavy, upholstered chair hanging from a fragile mini-blind in front of an unbroken window. Good humor and camaraderie helped everyone get through the arduous chores of cleaning up and rebuilding.

The two examples above represent *absurdity* and *incongruity,* two key ingredients of humor. For an example of the third key ingredient of humor, *exaggeration,* ask any middle-school teenager what happened to his homework. Listen for the three key ingredients; they can be found in everyday life. Almost any Change event can be "lightened up" by using one or more of these key ingredients, and doing so eases tension and places a happening in perspective. It's like taking the event in your fingers, holding it up to the light, and twisting it around to put the picture in a different light.

Memories of happy times can also transform a stressful time and put life into perspective. During the initial grief at my father's death, our Kansas minister asked us to remember some happy or funny times with Dad. It was easy, because he had been a tease and a jokester. We recalled how he had built a snow mountain in his yard for the school children to enjoy. They laughed as they walked by, for out of one side of the mountain stuck a head with a hat, and from the other side, suspended on sticks, was a pair of shoes. Was a man buried there? As time passed, the memory of his late Alzheimer's-affected years faded as we remembered the fun times we had shared. We gained perspective.

Good for Personal Health

Laughter is also good for health. It stimulates our bodies to perform better and makes endorphins that kill pain. Sister Angelica Menta, a humor consultant and stand-up comedy specialist in Houston, Texas, teaches people how to convert stress into laughter. She says, "Humor creates permanent stretch marks on the brain." Then she shows persons how to get those stretch marks.

Many of us are familiar with the pioneering work of well-known writer Norman Cousins, who treated his painful spondylitis with self-made prescriptions of humor by repeatedly watching the Marx brothers and other entertaining movies. His method of getting life into "lightened up" perspective helped relieve the stress of his painful illness and actually made him well. After his second book on the relationship of humor to healing, doctors and research scientists took up the cause and began serious study of why and how humor relates to the body. Today, a great body of research shows the enormous physical benefits of amusement.

But humor makes no promise of healing the physical body in everyone. It can transform a situation, entertain, renew the spirit, naturally release chemicals into the body, and cause emotional healing, but it makes no promise. That would be an exaggeration. The true wonder of amusement is that without promise of anything, it is celebration and lots of fun.

Good for Socialization

Not only does sharing a comedic moment benefit personal health, it also serves a social function by building bridges and breaking down barriers. The next time you go to a party or attend a meeting that opens with coffee time, listen for laughter, and you will find where people are congregated. They are drawn to each other in a place where they find entertainment, relaxation, and a leveling of status.

It also happens in traumatic situations. Two days after an apartment complex burned, when tenants were sifting, shoveling, and undertaking the grim task of finding any precious memory, one tenant walked along doing a strange thing. He stopped at each apartment and called an absurd question into the charred remains: "Are you having fun yet?" Each resident reacted the same way. A moment of disgusted silence was followed by a belly laugh. After a while, the residents took breaks and seemed to gravitate to the questioner. In a matter of minutes, each was sharing his or her story of loss, one of the first steps in trauma grief resolution. An hour later they were heard telling ridiculous stories about the surprising junk they had recovered, and they were all laughing. Humor brought them together, leveled them to a common denominator, and helped them socialize themselves into encouragement.

Mutual amusement also helps family and friends build bridges. Within this small group, inside jokes are born and perpetuated, a sort of "We're in the same club" atmosphere. In this club, jokes can replace blame (the imaginary cat, Charlie, always breaks the vase and spills the sugar—*absurdity*), good humor can replace criticism of the talkative great-aunt who is coming for a visit (Oh! You mean Aunt-Olive-of-the-closed-mouth?—*incongruity*), and arguments over chores get lightened

(Is this the 198th time you've emptied the dishwasher?—
exaggeration).

Humor Styles

Styles of humor vary with individuals. Some prefer cartoons
and jokes in solitude. These adults might be found in front of
the television, watching children's cartoons, or they may enjoy
chuckling to themselves over the brief jokes in a magazine. For
them, humor is private.

Others get the greatest enjoyment from hearing and telling
jokes. Healthy teasing may be part of their social interaction
with others, making them fun to be around. When they speak
in public, the interjected humor makes the speech easy to listen
to, and the audience settles back to learn from what is said.

Styles of humor vary with age groups, too. If the fast-moving
Change event in your life involves people of all ages, you have
probably already noticed that what is lighthearted, entertaining,
or funny for someone of a different age may seem bizarre to
you. Children especially grow through discovery periods in
humor that reflect their development. They outgrow bathroom
humor just as teenagers outgrow the cutting and frightening
humor that acts as a release valve for them and makes them feel
superior. Television humor affects all ages, with a family watching
the same thing but seeing comedy in varied ways. Somewhere
between childhood, the teen years, and adulthood our humor
usually changes into a more forgiving, less cutting, more
accepting style.

In her book *Compassionate Laughter, Jest for Your Health*,
registered nurse Patty Wooten writes of mature humor that
occurs after we come to terms with who we are.

> The humor of maturity is the ability to laugh at others
> and ourselves, as we all share common predicaments,
> embarrassments and temptations. Mature humor returns
> to the lighthearted playfulness of the child, but is no
> longer the playfulness of innocence. Rather, it is the

playfulness of one who has experienced suffering, but has not been conquered by it. We are able to laugh, be playful and lighthearted, in spite of, and in a sense because of the conflicts and disappointments of life. Adult humor emerges from a sense of harmony, peace, and liberation, and it is used to express our faith, love, hope and compassion.[16]

Except for humor that hurts or diminishes another person, all humor should be honored and tried. This is especially true for persons who must invent or reinvent it in order to get through trying situations. It's okay to flub punch lines as long as you try. It's okay to forget to mail the cartoon you cut out to send someone. It's okay to have a silly giggle or a stupid-sounding belly laugh. The main thing is to make an effort to lighten up, to learn to say yes, no, and whoopee, to discover a laughing spirit inside. It's there, and it can be found.

Beyond jokes and even words, the laughing spirit is the essence of natural mirth that connects all human hearts in an unspoken universal language of gentle delight. Humor of the laughing spirit includes all human beings, is never at the expense of an individual or group, and does not depend on cleverness or wit to be understood. The pleasant release of tension, the relief that causes us to smile or chuckle when we feel the presence of the laughing spirit, comes from the sudden realization that we are not separate from each other after all.[17]

The Theory of Relativity

Einstein may have thought up the theory of relativity in the field of physics, but it is nothing new to Christians. My personal theory of relativity has no complicated formula: What is, is, and God is with me. All happenings are relative to how I choose to meet them. I have heard people talk of the flip or good side to poverty, independence, health, and property. They say that all plans are relative to substitute plans that had to be made. During times of catastrophic happenings, we witness good coming from the situation. Having personal possessions snatched away relieves one of responsibility for them. Personally, I'd take the possessions, but what is, is, and it is related to how you meet the situation.

Most upsetting things are relative, that is, they have a negative side, but a positive side can be found. Here are some examples.

- Your home is destroyed by fire; however, you and your family are safe.
- The drug dog at school sniffs out cocaine in the locker next to yours. You do not use drugs, but feared the smell had seeped into your locker. It hadn't, so you say thanks to God.
- A gang shoots up your son's car. The shotgun blast rips a hole in the side of his car in front of the gas tank and slams through the driver's seat, missing him by less than an inch. The car's a mess, you have $500 deductible, and he is shaking—but safe. After you have looked at the hole and have stopped shaking, you give thanks that his life was spared.
- You have been diagnosed with diabetes. However, a nutritionist teaches you how to eat, and a technician shows you how to administer insulin. It's a bad news, good news sort of situation. You choose health and move on with your life.
- A tornado removes your place of business during the night, but no employees were injured. As a bonus of good luck, you find the insurance papers.
- After years of being plagued by nightmarish memories of a World War II battle in which in real life you were the only survivor, you are finally able to share the burden with another veteran. The nightmares decrease,

but the memories are still there. You begin the process of healing that will allow you to celebrate your life, and you give thanks for possibilities of the future.

Look at New Possibilities

What if the problem can't be cured, won't go away, and doesn't seem to have any relative good? This seldom happens, but when it does, it's a bummer. Trouble is relative to how you choose to meet it, and you have to learn to live with it. This calls for new knowledge, new skills, and deliberately choosing to reinvent the ways you will meet the problem. Think of problems as opportunities as you bask in the love of God and do what you have to do.

> Though I walk in the midst of trouble,
> you preserve me against the wrath of my enemies;
> you stretch out your hand,
> and your right hand delivers me.
> The Lord will fulfill his purpose for me;
> your steadfast love, O Lord, endures forever.
> Do not forsake the work of your hands. (Ps. 138:7–8)

The Hem of His Garment

Have you ever tried to get the autograph of a famous person? Caught in the frenzy of pushers and shovers and the clamor of yelling for attention, you *almost* made it to the inner rim where a famous person would sign his name. Then suddenly, the celebrity turned his back and moved away from you. You shoved and stretched until your hand touched the back of his jacket. Forever imprinted in your mind is the feel of the smooth leather jacket, and shaped on your heart is one thought: "I touched him!" So great was his influence that you may even feel that he touched you, and in a way, he did, or at least he had already done so; that's why you were reaching out.

The same seeking and animated fervor used by autograph fans can be directed toward Jesus. In fact, there are exciting reports of it in the Bible:

> He came down with them and stood on a level place, with a great crowd of his disciples and a great multitude of people from all Judea, Jerusalem, and the coast of Tyre and Sidon. They had come to hear him and to be healed of their diseases; and those who were troubled with unclean spirits were cured. And all in the crowd were trying to touch him, for power came out from him and healed all of them. (Lk. 6:17–19)

Mark tells of a woman with an illness who was in a large crowd pressing around Jesus.

> She had heard about Jesus, and came up behind him in the crowd and touched his cloak, for she said, "If I but touch his clothes, I will be made well." Immediately her hemorrhage stopped; and she felt in her body that she was healed of her disease. Immediately aware that power had gone forth from him, Jesus turned about in the crowd and said, "Who touched my clothes?" And his disciples said to him, "You see the crowd pressing in on you; how can you say, 'Who touched me?'"He looked all around to see who had done it. But the woman, knowing what had happened to her, came in fear and trembling, fell down before him,and told him the whole truth. He said to her, "Daughter, your faith has made you well; go in peace, and be healed of your disease." (Mk. 5:27–34)

> And wherever he went, into villages or cities or farms, they laid the sick in the marketplaces, and begged him that they might touch even the fringe of his cloak; and all who touched it were healed. (Mk. 6:56)

We can feel the same seeking and animated fervor used to gain autographs as we reach toward Jesus. Oh! To touch him and have him touch us! But only in our imaginations can we touch a garment that Jesus is wearing. So, is anything wrong with imagination? After all these years, he still lives. After all these years, we still have faith. It still happens today! Supernatural healing does take place. We know of these instances and praise God for them.

However, great disappointment can come if touching the edge of Jesus' cloak doesn't bring instant healing of our situation. What happens to our daring faith when we reach out expectantly and there is no apparent healing of our body or hurting situation? There are as many individualized answers as persons in the next mile. I believe that there are many ways of being healed, and some of them we have never considered. I also believe that healing of a situation or an illness can come through a process that may take time.

Processes

In the age of instant pudding, instant grits, and instant everything, it is hard to wrap our minds around what may be a process, one that may be extremely slow and not instantly apparent. The person who, with faith, patiently perseveres will eventually realize life-changing presence and can look back to witness the way touching the hem has sustained and improved any situation. Hearing stories of wholeness and healing can give us clues about how the processing may work. Keep in mind that this process works differently in individual cases.

THE PROCESS OF SOMETHING BETTER:

In the midst of a sticky divorce from an abusive husband, Linda truly expected God to reform her husband and make it possible for her marriage to be saved. Distressed over God's apparent inactivity on her behalf, she persevered in prayer, kept her faith, and discovered blessings in her new life. She found that healing became a time-consuming, natural process that eventually led her through new doors to a fuller life.

THE PROCESS OF INTEGRATION:

Walt wasn't sick, had no huge Change event in his life. He just had an eternal discontent with himself that made him feel fragmented into little pieces. He felt like Humpty Dumpty, who fell off the wall—all the king's horses and all the king's men couldn't put him together again. But someone could. As Walt reached toward the hem of Jesus' cloak on a daily basis, he began a subtle tilt in a new direction. His recognition that he was a beloved child of God, whether in small pieces or integrated, helped him see other people in the same light. It put balance in his life by showing him that he wasn't the center of the universe but was an important part of it. The tilt of the new direction helped him toward a positive attitude toward life, and surprisingly, he found more zest in living, even in the midst of joy and sorrow or understanding and puzzlement.

THE PROCESS OF WELLNESS:

Satcho had lived with her grandfather on the Navajo reservation all her life. After his diagnosis of cancer and the prediction that he had only a short time to live, Satcho felt that her heart would break. How could she live without the wise man who treated her with such tenderness? She prayed for health for the old man, sat by his hospital bed, watched him suffer in his stoic way, then listened to his last breath. She felt sick inside. It took months of outer and inner wailing to complete her cycle of grief. Gradually, the wailing and sickness inside her subsided, and she felt its burden laid aside. Then she was able to say prayers of thanksgiving for her own wellness.

Satcho made a friend while in the hospital. His name was Louisville, but she called him Louie for short, especially because he had leukemia. After her grandfather died, Satcho visited Louie. Instead of the pale, thin boy she had known weeks before,

Louie looked hearty. She was puzzled. "My prayers were answered," he told her. "They found a new treatment!" Satcho hugged Louie, but in her mind was a question, "Why are life and death such mysteries?"

THE PROCESS OF WHOLENESS:

Hakeem knew that he was different from the time he was taken out of first grade and placed in a special school. He couldn't talk, and if he did, the words exploded out of his mouth sounding like mashed coughs. As he grew older, he tried harder and harder to say what he was thinking, but classmates made fun of him. His neighbor, who baby-sat him, treated him like a piece of stone even though he scribbled notes and tried to please her. By the time he was a teenager, he knew that he was not only different but worthless and a burden to everyone. When his aunt came from overseas to live with his family, he discovered a new kind of love, for she taught him about her God and told him that God loved him and had always loved him, even when he didn't know it. Such a surprise made Hakeem scramble for paper and write an exclamation mark on it. As his aunt taught him to love God back, Hakeem felt that all the parts of his life were glued together and under a new light. He felt whole.

All Children

Mental development, skin color, face shapes, beliefs, economic status, marital status, and many other characteristics make us different from one another. Yet we as children of God are alike. The woman who touched the hem of Jesus' cloak broke Jewish law by doing so. Jewish law forbade a menstruating woman from touching anyone, yet she had the audacity to touch the Christ. The story of Jesus' response forever banishes the idea that certain people, because they are different, should be shunned.

In a realm beyond what we understand, many persons are not physically healed as the woman in the Bible story was, but we can learn to live in a wounding situation with the touch of

Jesus as our sustainer, comforter, and hope. It would be much more comforting if we could actually touch Jesus and feel the power emanating from him, but he is not physically touchable. However (there's always a however), we can get in touch, feel in touch, and stay in touch with the healing heart of Jesus. We can feel his presence and realize his blessings as we pick our way through the maze of events that have made our lives and sometimes our selves "different."

Milling

Thirty-six canoeists meet at the campgrounds next to the cold, fast river in the frosty October dawn. They unload their canoes, don wet gear, and help one another equip their boats. Shivering, they share hot coffee packed in a variety of insulated bottles before dawn. They begin part one of milling as the group breaks down into smaller units, hailing and hugging old acquaintances and welcoming newcomers. People begin to mill around, moving in mass confusion yet mass order. Finally, each is attached to a group that provides information he or she needs or a group in which she or he can share knowledge of canoeing. Some ask, How far is it to the first take-out? Others ask, Where are the rapids and are they category two or six? What are the marker names of the falls or rocks on this river? (Some names include Meat Grinder, Body Snatcher, Boat Bender, Death Wish Rapid, or Widow Maker.) Sometimes the old-timers recite the names of the rocks and falls to make newcomers cautious; sometimes it's to scare them to death. More milling takes place as persons encourage and challenge one another, and it continues until each of the thirty-six persons has sorted into a traveling group, a shuttle driver, and a take-out place. Although milling may have looked like camaraderie and confusion, it was much more. It really was sharing and similarity sorting.

Part two of milling comes at the end of that day of paddling, after all the shuttles have returned laden with dripping boats and tired people in high spirits. It's an explosion of stories about rescues, new things learned, and terror on certain rapids, of inside jokes and lots of teasing and laughing, and, of course, of hugs. Persons who were encouraged or challenged at the earlier milling are sought out to be congratulated or consoled. Did they make it over Death Wish Rapid, or did they portage? How was the rest of the day? Did the new paddle handle as well as advertised? Did they like the new kneeling pads? Time slips by, and someone builds a fire as darkness falls. Milling fades down as people change clothes or prepare food.

The Importance of Similarity

Milling occurs in almost any activity where people with similar interests congregate as they search for soul mates or information or as they renew acquaintances. In skiing, it's called après-ski. Ministers mill at church conferences. Teachers mill at training conferences, partly for renewed friendships and partly in search of new ideas and techniques. In a similar manner, persons who find themselves in situations that call for unexpected and far-reaching changes benefit from finding a group with similar interests. Sometimes called focus or support groups, the groups function as a forum for sharing and discussing a topic of mutual interest, whether it's alcoholism, divorce, grief for a family member, a specific illness, or learning together how to live with a person with mental illness. Caregivers find support groups a safe place for discussion of their emotions and fatigue, and parents of developmentally delayed children learn from and encourage one another.

There's a lot to milling or support groups that is unexplainable, unplanned, just a gut feeling of need to be with someone who understands. In a framework of honesty and respect, such a group is a comfortable place to relax.

When you join a support group, you take the gift of yourself to meetings. At ease in a group, you can share what you have learned and learn what will be shared. Someone there, perhaps many persons, will welcome a newcomer to lifestyle adaptation or reinvention. They have either been there or are walking your same road.

Where can you find a support group? Look on bulletin boards and in newspapers, listen to the grapevine, ask your friends, or see if your church hosts meetings. If your church doesn't have a group, ask for permission to form one along the lines of your needs. Or if you have three friends adjusting to fast-change events, invite them to lunch and suggest that they start a group. Milling, a concept of similarity and fellowship, doesn't require thirty-six cold canoeists; two or three persons with like needs gathered in a cozy room drinking coffee can form a positive group. My friend, a widow and survivor of her husband's long-term illness, shared her time and the wisdom she had accrued in taking care of her husband. Two friends whose husbands were in a nursing home became her mission outreach. They formed a trio support group that became a haven for all three. They didn't call it a caregiver's support group; it was three friends enjoying one another.

Although all types of support groups are valuable and may offer good, specific information, church groups usually have the backing of a loving and accepting congregation. Large churches can offer more specific groups, such as those for depression, grief, sandwich generation caregiving, addiction, divorce recovery, children in divorce, cancer, or other chronic illnesses. Smaller churches can easily amass enough people to have a group focused on stressful events in general and may have needs that change. Both types of groups can offer time for what I call a gift exchange of information, plus specific aids in the form of outside specialists who inform and lead discussions. The following are some suggested topics:

Grief as a tool for moving on, the adventure of adjusting your lifestyle, life detours, finding glue for self-esteem, things I can do now that I can't do what I used to do, adaptive living strategies, caregivers speak up, the dynamics of friendship during stressful events, planning for the future, violence directed at children and youth, where to find financial aid, new directions in recreation, visualization as a tool to reality, defining my family role, how to get what you need and want without getting mad, how to travel, humor and health, dealing with depression, tips for saving energy, theology when the answer is no, adapting ways you worship, personal power over a situation, preventing poverty of the soul.

When a congregation offers support or focus groups, its members are speaking a special language of loving inclusion. They are saying, we are your oasis; we love you, need you, and seek your participation. If no such group exists, the members may think that someone has taken care of you. Do something positive. Start your own group.

7

Reinventing the
CALL TO SERVICE

No reinvented life is complete without provision for helping others, and no form of service is too small or too large. From raising money for a worthy cause by running a marathon, donating a new wing for the library, or building a Habitat house to folding flyers, praying for someone, listening patiently to someone's troubles, or telephoning a list, each service moment is important.

The act of helping others serves several outstanding purposes for the reinventor. First, doing for someone other than ourselves changes our perspective when we fade into the background and focus elsewhere. Second, in doing for others, we discover that we are needed, a blessing to our self-esteem. Third, when we answer God's call to abandon selfish acts, we also reenact the example of servanthood given by Jesus.

Mayday! Mayday!

The noise of the air battle fought over enemy territory was deafening, and the blue sky became obscured by black smoke and red flames. Planes burned. Bodies hung limply from strafed parachutes. A voice crackled over the airwaves, "Mayday! Mayday! Larry. 610." Two fighters darted toward 610, then hovered nearby as a lone parachute exploded from the plane and drifted toward the ground. When an enemy plane zoomed in to kill Larry, one of the fighters swooshed down with rapid firing. Minutes later, 610 exploded in mid-air, and burning parts drifted silently down. Larry disappeared into the woods below, and the fighters fled to higher altitude.

Years later, Larry, volunteering in a hospice, recalled his "Mayday! Mayday! Larry. 610" story for a young man who kept profusely thanking him for his help. "I'm just passing it on," Larry said. "My buddies put their lives on the line for me to keep me from being strafed," he said. "They took their eyes off themselves long enough to save my life."

The Last Straw

The term *Mayday* signals the last straw, no place to go and no way out. It is derived from the French term *m'aidez*, meaning "help me," or *venez m'aider*, meaning "come, help me." Many persons forced to reinvent their lives because of life-shaking events receive help from friends, family, support groups, doctors, lawyers, mentors, or even strangers who answer the call "come, help me" for people who haven't even asked for help. They intuitively recognize *m'aidez* and turn to support the needy.

Perhaps all of us who have been aided and have lived through hard times must take our eyes off ourselves and look to the needs of others. One of Jesus' most vivid parables teaches us about responding to need in direct, simple ways.

> "For I was hungry and you gave me food, I was thirsty
> and you gave me something to drink, I was a stranger

and you welcomed me, I was naked and you gave me clothing, I was sick and you took care of me, I was in prison and you visited me." (Mt. 25:35–36)

The parable continues with the concept that whatever we do or don't do for those he has mentioned, we do or don't do for him.

Some of the things we are to notice in people around us are loneliness, grief, anger, bitterness, sickness, hunger, or exhausting fatigue. When we become aware of the needs of those around us and make loving responses, we are put in touch with Jesus.

In the midst of having our own needs met, we can minister to others if we take our eyes off ourselves. Not only will it add beauty to our lives and put life in perspective, it may save us from our selfish selves.

You Want Me to Do *What?*
(*or:* Visions! Who Needs Them?)

The eighth-century prophets Amos, Hosea, Isaiah, and Micah are, for me, some of the most intriguing characters in the Bible. Why? Perhaps it's because I first studied them at a period in my life when I felt freshly called to a life of service for the church. I could identify with their idealism, the visionary acts, and the preachments.

And perhaps it was because the teacher of my eighth-century prophets class, also the dean of the university, loved the Old Testament and especially the prophets. He had a flair for dramatizing them.

Well, he had a flair for the dramatic even in the way he began class. His students could do imitations of him opening class: Hurry into classroom, take off coat (silently we'd count 2-3-4), roll up sleeves (2-3-4), loosen collar button (2-3-4), flip up necktie (2-3-4), sigh (2-3-4), and say, "Let's get to work!" He did it every day, semester after semester.

Perhaps it was because the prophets turned him on that he did dramatic imitations of them. Climbing on an overturned wooden soft-drink crate, he began Amos' speech in which he tells the Israelites what they want to hear just to get their attention. He tells them about the bad luck of their enemies—and then starts in on *them*. Amos was a psychologist as well as a visionary. I tried his technique on a group of counselors once, and I was a dismal failure. Perhaps I needed the wooden crate. Or a flipped necktie.

Amos was a traveling man who collected information, mixed it with what he knew of God, and verbalized his vision of the future to the right audience. There were many biblical people with this intelligent foresight. Some—Isaiah, for example—literally had supernatural visions.

My mind recalls others who had great pictures in their heads and hearts of what they wanted to accomplish. Remember Francis of Asissi? He left the lavish home of his wealthy parents wearing a rope belt over his tunic, a symbol of his dream that he wanted to be with and for the poor. Another visionary was William Henry Seward, the secretary of state who wanted to make Alaska part of the United States. He persevered until finally purchasing it from Russia for two cents an acre, a lot of money then. People laughed and called it "Seward's Ice Box" or "Seward's Folly." With Alaska now a thriving state, people have forgotten how they laughed at what they thought was Seward's joke.

Thomas Edison envisioned electric lights. Martin Luther King, Jr., had unusual competence in discerning equality by peaceful means. In every community there have been people of vision who founded orphanages, homes for unwed mothers, clinics for HIV patients, apartment complexes for elderly persons, safe havens for persons who have been abused, and respite care for parents with children needing special handling. Others conceived the idea of Habitat for Humanity, medevac flights, international physician exchange programs. The individuals with dreams or visions persevered until each vision became reality.

There's an old saying, "Without vision, the people perish." Then someone added, "With the wrong vision, they perish anyway." So what can we do with "aha!" experiences, unusual perceptions, or visions that come to us? Sometimes they are fleeting. But if they're persistent, we are called to deal with them. Unless the vision comes engraved in stone or in loud voices with witnesses or in a burning bush, we have to figure out what to do. We have to scratch our heads and think and question, perhaps even develop tests for ourselves to discover which are worthy visions and dreams and which are passing fancies.

Persistent prayer sifts a persistent vision from fancy or folly. Sifting the purpose through God's Word can also give us knowledge. We can also ask ourselves if the vision tests out against facts, but sometimes God's wishes fly in the face of fact, making no sense at all. At this point, an amazed and perhaps disbelieving person might say, "You want me to do *what?*" and continue down the path of processing the idea.

The processing may mean translating your idea through sharing it with someone and listening to feedback. Sometimes you might look for fertile ground and sow ideas where they can grow. Or the idea may not have timely merit, and it withers. If they don't wither but stay alive, most visions then go through the refining and sifting of compromise as others tag their interpretations or dreams on to yours. Sometimes when your vision comes to fruition, it barely resembles what you started toward, but it has become enriched by the creativity and wisdom of others.

James 3:13–18 gives guidelines not only for testing the purpose of an intelligent foresight or vision but also for the way it can be brought to fruition:

> Who is wise and understanding among you? Show by
> your good life that your works are done with gentleness
> born of wisdom. But if you have bitter envy and selfish
> ambition in your hearts, do not be boastful and false to
> the truth. Such wisdom does not come down from above,

but is earthly, unspiritual, devilish. For where there is envy and selfish ambition, there will also be disorder and wickedness of every kind. But the wisdom from above is first pure, then peaceable, gentle, willing to yield, full of mercy and good fruits, without a trace of partiality or hypocrisy. And a harvest of righteousness is sown in peace for those who make peace.

What's Your Vision?

What is your vision? Has a turning point in your life caused you to reinvent your lifestyle? Has a crisis in your life shown you a need that has burned a hole in your soul? Are you ready and willing to share that need so that someone can dream with you? Is there a persistent inclination to do something that you keep trying to ignore? It's time to listen up, recognize it, share it, sift it, test it, and perhaps get to work.

A rock pile ceases to be a rock pile the moment a single man contemplates it, bearing within him the image of a cathedral.[18]

The Power to Be

Everyone has periods in life when the ebb and flow of activities changes from fast to slow or even stops:

- You break a leg.
- Divorce renders you numb and unmovable.
- You have extended flu, maybe even pneumonia.
- You have cancer.
- You are too depressed to get out of bed.
- Your active body suddenly lets you down; you don't know your own body.
- Your employer closes its doors.
- A loved one dies.

- Your church lets you down.
- A friend wounds you.
- Everything happens at once, and old coping skills fail.

These or other events overtake us. It's a moment we all dread—a spiral of trouble paralyzes the will. *Inactivity* takes charge. Sometimes the spiral is so small we are taken by surprise in the paralysis. We had no idea it would affect us that way. How can it be? No play. No work. No good deeds. No bad deeds. Alteration in life's progress seems to take over, and there is no road map of what to do next. Stopped cold inside a little box, we find that new boundaries twist and turn our plans for the future!

Trying to sort out inactivity brings echoes of scripture we learned in Sunday school:

But be *doers* of the word, and not merely hearers (Jas. 1:22). *(How* can *I do?)*

I can *do* all things through him who strengthens me (Phil. 4:13). *(Hurry up and strengthen me, God, so I can get on with it!)*

Suddenly, inactivity, a physical and mental freeze-up, becomes a theological as well as a physical challenge. What about feeding the hungry? visiting the lonely? giving water to the thirsty? (Mt. 25:35). Verses you have previously understood require new thought. You mentally scratch the inside of your head and read them again in the light of what is happening to you.

Perhaps this head scratching is a nudge and an opportunity for spiritual growth. Here is the chance, if not the mandate, to *be*. As a child of God (1 Jn. 3:1a), just be. Be where you are. Be who you are at the moment. It's okay to just be and not be doing for someone else but for God's lovable person—you. Be good to yourself. Sit. Lie motionless. Stand somewhere. Spend two hours studying a lily. Sit for three hours listening to a wren recite its repertoire. Rest in yourself. Rest in the Lord.

Good news! A permission slip from God to just *be* makes it possible to cease frantic striving and to rest in the Lord. Just rest.

In addition, here are a few "inactivity mental exercises" that I have tried. They have helped me practice the power of *be*-ing in another way:

- Read Psalm 23. *Be* a sheep. Your shepherd watches over you while you eat, while you sleep, while you jump and kick up your heels in joy, while you drink, while you hurt. When other sheep in your family grieve or suffer, God, the shepherd, keeps watch, walks with them to the sheepfold, and watches them overnight.

- Read Mark 16. *Be* a big rock. Imagine just sitting next to the open tomb. At the moment you can't run down the road to tell people that Jesus is risen. Just sit there and *be*. Be in awe that the tomb is empty, or just *be* a rock. Be what you can. Feel whatever you feel.

- Read 1 Corinthians 1:4–9. *Be* yourself with whatever ebb and flow of change has washed over you. When you read scripture, notice what it does *not* say. For example: notice that the first line of scripture, "I give thanks to my God always for you because of the grace of God that has been given you in Christ Jesus," does *not* say, "I give thanks to my God always for those of you who are not ill, not divorced, not widowed, not depressed, not homeless…"

The thanksgiving of which Paul spoke is for you exactly as you are. You are entitled to *be* wherever you are in whatever condition you are, tuning in so that Christ may strengthen you in your *be*-ing.

Recliner Reinvention

Letha taught Sunday school, led a prayer group, and helped people in the community get their roofs fixed or their children fed or whatever it took to be God's love let loose in the world. She worked in her husband's business, raised a family, and grew a garden every year.

The last time I saw her, she could barely rise from the recliner in her living room. Nothing could stop the arthritic stiffening and swelling that made it too painful to navigate the garden or work on her beloved community projects. But neither could anything stop the glowing spirit that welcomed friends to her home. Twice a week it was a Bible study group that came to her home. She led, of course. Sometimes it was a down-and-out woman with no place to go who stayed a few nights. More often she welcomed someone with a thirsty soul who wanted to hear what Letha had to say about Jesus. Often it was friends like me who had moved away and wandered back to visit with the woman who had helped us with struggles of the soul and stomach. She had fed me when the budget was flat.

I call Letha's late-in-life ministry the recliner reinvention. With her attitude of humility and her face reflecting the light of the partnership she had formed with God, it became natural for people to seek Letha and sit next to her recliner.

Letha moved into disability and old age as naturally as she clung to her faith through trials. Did she grieve over abilities lost? Probably. Did she resent her inability to *go* places and *do* things? Probably. But I never heard of it, because she had reinvented her call to service. Apparently, in her thinking, God wanted her to be where she was, and because she never did anything without talking to "Heem" about it, she knew that her ministry would be wherever she had the energy to sit. Gradually, the maroon recliner became that place. She made accommodations in her lifestyle, her time and place of worship, her holidays, and her call to service—not through "cutting back" on physical activity or just getting by, but in searching for ways to wrestle every ounce of zest out of her daily life. The testimonies to this zest were her sparkling eyes and broad smile and the exciting yet peaceful way she lived her life for "Heem."

Letha didn't have labels for attitude adjustment or lifestyle change and reinvention. Using scripture, intuition, dreams, vision, and leadings of the Holy Spirit, Letha had the courage of an open mind and years of experience with God to adjust by doing what came naturally. She had been redefining her theology and who she was for most of her life. Now the richness of doing that bore fruit.

Many of her friends fell into statistical tables. One friend was one of the 50,000 persons a year who become blind. Eight friends, ranging from childhood to adult, were developmentally delayed.[19] Two of them married. Thirty percent of the members of her precious congregation developed a chronic illness. Three developed hearing loss. One suffered brain injury. One committed suicide, and Letha counseled the remaining spouse. Seven became divorced. Three lost their homes to fire or flood. Six or seven were separated from loved ones by death. For these and others who were persons rather than statistics, Letha was a caring person and role model who took to heart Paul's advice to the church at Philippi,

> Let each of you look not to your own interests, but to the interests of others. Let the same mind be in you that was in Christ Jesus. (Phil. 2:4–5)

Around me for my whole life have been and are role models for reinventing life, people who took time in service in their communities, people who didn't always know that they were role models.

Hazel and Joe

The first month after retirement, Hazel and Joe (my parents) participated in the usual potluck dinners and bingo games. By the second month, lethargy had overtaken them; they felt empty. By the third month Hazel had volunteered to baby-sit at the bloodmobile, Joe was helping repair and build churches in the area, and both of them were delivering Meals-on-Wheels. Usefulness, a tool in reinventing new direction in life, made them feel fulfilled.

Maureen

A talented painter whose portraits brought top money in a large American city, Maureen had been teased for years with questions such as, "Do you paint garages and barns?" and "Can you do my front porch next week?" For some reason the questions didn't anger her as they did her famous painter friends, so when she became ill with multiple sclerosis and could no longer paint portraits, it seemed natural to try her shaking hands at exterior painting.

Slowly her back steps bloomed with green and red; the ramp her family built turned the color of waving wheat fields; and the inside of her bedroom door sported wavy-line checks and dots of yellow and blue. Fatigue, her constant enemy, made her reconsider commercial house and design painting as a career, but she volunteered to help paint houses for Habitat for Humanity. Every weekend, as she was able, Maureen advised on color and wielded a paintbrush. A diverted gift, often the mark of reinvention, can help fill a need in the community.

> Now there are varieties of gifts, but the same Spirit; and there are varieties of services, but the same Lord; and there are varieties of activities, but it is the same God who activates all of them in everyone. (1 Cor. 12:4–6)

Fred

Fred can't move his body. He is the victim of a drive-by shooting that left him paralyzed. When the leaves outside begin to drift past his window, he imagines his football buddies practicing for the next crucial game. More and more since the accident, Fred has been using his mind in a new way so that he can remember without keeping notes. When the crucial football date approaches, Fred pictures each player and number and prays for that person's well-being and sportsmanship.

Yasuko

"God needs casseroles," Yasuko told me. "Right now I'm unemployed and have time to cook." She devised a plan for learning the names of persons who, because of illness or financial problems, might welcome something good to eat. Yasuko is a fantastic cook. A simple casserole ceases to be a casserole the moment it becomes God's work.

Sam

Sam, an energetic retired minister of the gospel, had traveled to Russia as a mission coordinator. Conditions there appalled him. After his official retirement, he "retired" to his workshop to build birdhouses, which he sold to make money for mission work in Russia. His birdhouses are sold at local mission stores and community boutiques and have brought hundreds of dollars. The birdhouses are a small part of the service in which Sam and his wife, Beverly, are involved. They retired in order to travel frequently to Russia, where they have helped start churches and have inspired American groups to undertake projects in orphanages there. Each willingly serves in unexpected ways.

Retirement—early or otherwise—becomes a main event in life, requiring a change in lifestyle and in the ways persons spend their time, energy, and money. Service to others can enrich the years of "chronological enhancement" and can open doors of the mind and heart for persons of any age who face stressing events. Most faiths, including the Christian faith, place special value on serving ministries, and the persons who get involved in them are surprised to discover that helping and sharing fills them with deep, inner joy.

Discovering such deep, inner joy marks a reinvented person.

Postscript:
LIFE'S HEADACHES

It was just a headache, but it went on and on, getting more blinding and explosive for weeks. Then suddenly, just when my reinvented life had seemed to be going smoothly, I woke up in intensive care at a local hospital after cranial surgery.

Oh, no! Not another junkyard experience!

The first words I remember were spoken by a nurse walking past the foot of my little cubicle, speaking to another nurse acoss a hallway. She said, "I'm going down to the morgue." I gasped, then realized, "She's not taking me, so I must be alive."

Oh, yes! Something to celebrate, and celebration can't be oversold.

But here I am again in one of life's messes. Nothing works on me but my mouth, and it works in slow motion. I feel like I'm an exile in a new land where I can't speak the language.

Oh, yes! It's definitely a new life junkyard experience.

Well, I never try to reclaim a junk situation alone. I fly to an awesome God who loves me. I try to talk to God with my mind, but the words get lost and tangled in my irritated brain. I grope for connections, and come up with "Rest in the Lord," and "Be still and know that I am God," and "Emmanuel, God with me." Later, stillness comes to me as I listen to classical music on a little earphone cassette player brought by my daughter. I relax into the calm and rest in the Lord.

Oh, yes! I'll definitely have to retune worship. It will take time.

A month later, awed by my speedy progress, I take time to look backward to discover that I used my mother's triage questions on pieces brought home from the Kansas junkyard: What will you do with it? My answer was, "Work to the future."

Her other question, "Who will help you?" appeared to have an answer too big to explain. My surgeon and a great team of doctors, my wonderful family, my husband who held my hand through the whole time, a bevy of nurses and therapists, and literally hundreds of persons praying for me. Also helping me was a God I trusted to hold me in steadfast love, live or die

Yes, with help, I must definitely work to reinvent a life that can soar again. I don't have to do it alone. I'm in partnership with everyone who will help my body, heart, and spirit.

Everybody's Headaches

We all need help with our bodies, hearts, and spirits when events of change stop us dead in our tracks. These events—akin to some of life's biggest headaches from custody battles, huge personal disappointments, to homelessness or loss of vision— challenge us to new strategies and understandings.

Life's headaches keep turning up for everyone, most of them not excised by a surgeon. Some turmoil headache events will be cured, some must be borne covered with bandages, and others will be laid painfully in the open for the world to see. Some will allow us to rise like the phoenix from ashes. Some headaches will be cured or abated by plodding perseverence and reframing the event, that is, holding it up to the light of God for a new perspective. Others will simply see us propped in a chair or lying in bed looking out the window watching the seasons roll by in a time of laying-by, resting in God's calm inner fields. We have been promised that God is with us (Matthew 1:23), and we can learn that God walked in our past...and runs in our future.

NOTES

INTRODUCTION

[1]*Inventions and Discoveries* (Facts on File, 460 Park Ave South, New York, NY 10016, 1992), 92.

[2]*The Smithsonian Book of Inventions* (New York: Smithsonian Books, 1978), 82, 93.

CHAPTER I

[3]Ann Rose Davie and Ginny Thornburgh, *That All May Worship, An Interfaith Welcome to People with Disabilities* (National Organization on Disability, 910 16th Street, N. W., Suite 600, Washington, DC 20006, 1992), iii.

CHAPTER 2

[4]Ilene Morof Lubkin, *Chronic Illness Impact and Interventions* (Boston: Jones and Bartlett, 1986), 173.

[5]Ibid., 174–78. Classification of stages 2, 3, 4, and 5 are expanded from stages reported by Ilene Morof Lubkin. The sixth stage is one I presented in an earlier unpublished essay, "Hey! It's My Body!" (1996).

[6]Naomi Mitchum, "Haven't I Met You Somewhere Before?" Unpublished collection (1991).

[7]Carol A. Kelleher, *Good News Now,* vol. 3, no. 3 (Associated Catholic Charities of the Diocese of Galveston-Houston, 3520 Montrose Blvd., P. O. Box 66508, Houston, TX 77266, September 1998), 5.

CHAPTER 3

[8]Saint Patrick, Ireland, fifth century, translated by Cecil Frances Alexander.

[9]Naomi Mitchum, *More Fun with Drama* (Nashville: Abingdon Press, 1993), 44. Based on Psalm 25.

CHAPTER 4

[10]Fred Pratt Green, "God Is Here!" (1978).

[11]Dag Hammarskjold, *Markings,* trans. Leif Sjoberg and W. H. Auden (New York: Albert S. Knopf, 1964), 124.

[12]Lynda S. Paladin, *Ceremonies for Change, Creating Personal Ritual to Heal Life's Hurts* (Walpole, N. H.: Stillpoint Publishing, 1991), 40–45.

CHAPTER 6

[13]Traditional African American spiritual.

[14]Ibid.

[15]As quoted in Bruce Larson, *The Meaning and Mystery of Being Human* (Waco, Tex.: Word Books, 1978), 25.

[16]Patty Wooten, *Compassionate Laughter, Jest for Your Health* (Salt Lake City: Commune—A Key Publishing, 1996), 165.

[17]Ibid.

CHAPTER 7

[18]Antoine de Saint-Exupery, quoted in William Bridges, *Managing Transitions, Making the Most of Change* (Reading, Mass.: Addison-Wesley, 1991), 56.

[19]One of every ten Americans has a family member with mental retardation. Ninety percent are unchurched. "Introduction to Mental Retardation" (Arlington, Tex.: Association for Retarded Citizens National Headquarters News Bulletin, 1991), 1.

INDEX OF TOPICS

INDEX OF SCRIPTURE